EVALUATING THE EXPORT-IMPORT BANK IN THE GLOBAL ECONOMY

HEARING

BEFORE THE

SUBCOMMITTEE ON TERRORISM, NONPROLIFERATION, AND TRADE

OF THE

COMMITTEE ON FOREIGN AFFAIRS HOUSE OF REPRESENTATIVES

ONE HUNDRED FOURTEENTH CONGRESS

FIRST SESSION

OCTOBER 23, 2015

Serial No. 114–102

Printed for the use of the Committee on Foreign Affairs

Available via the World Wide Web: http://www.foreignaffairs.house.gov/ or http://www.gpo.gov/fdsys/

U.S. GOVERNMENT PUBLISHING OFFICE

97–269PDF   WASHINGTON : 2015

COMMITTEE ON FOREIGN AFFAIRS

EDWARD R. ROYCE, California, *Chairman*

CHRISTOPHER H. SMITH, New Jersey
ILEANA ROS-LEHTINEN, Florida
DANA ROHRABACHER, California
STEVE CHABOT, Ohio
JOE WILSON, South Carolina
MICHAEL T. McCAUL, Texas
TED POE, Texas
MATT SALMON, Arizona
DARRELL E. ISSA, California
TOM MARINO, Pennsylvania
JEFF DUNCAN, South Carolina
MO BROOKS, Alabama
PAUL COOK, California
RANDY K. WEBER SR., Texas
SCOTT PERRY, Pennsylvania
RON DeSANTIS, Florida
MARK MEADOWS, North Carolina
TED S. YOHO, Florida
CURT CLAWSON, Florida
SCOTT DesJARLAIS, Tennessee
REID J. RIBBLE, Wisconsin
DAVID A. TROTT, Michigan
LEE M. ZELDIN, New York
DANIEL DONOVAN, New York

ELIOT L. ENGEL, New York
BRAD SHERMAN, California
GREGORY W. MEEKS, New York
ALBIO SIRES, New Jersey
GERALD E. CONNOLLY, Virginia
THEODORE E. DEUTCH, Florida
BRIAN HIGGINS, New York
KAREN BASS, California
WILLIAM KEATING, Massachusetts
DAVID CICILLINE, Rhode Island
ALAN GRAYSON, Florida
AMI BERA, California
ALAN S. LOWENTHAL, California
GRACE MENG, New York
LOIS FRANKEL, Florida
TULSI GABBARD, Hawaii
JOAQUIN CASTRO, Texas
ROBIN L. KELLY, Illinois
BRENDAN F. BOYLE, Pennsylvania

AMY PORTER, *Chief of Staff*   THOMAS SHEEHY, *Staff Director*
JASON STEINBAUM, *Democratic Staff Director*

———

SUBCOMMITTEE ON TERRORISM, NONPROLIFERATION, AND TRADE

TED POE, Texas, *Chairman*

JOE WILSON, South Carolina
DARRELL E. ISSA, California
PAUL COOK, California
SCOTT PERRY, Pennsylvania
REID J. RIBBLE, Wisconsin
LEE M. ZELDIN, New York

WILLIAM KEATING, Massachusetts
BRAD SHERMAN, California
BRIAN HIGGINS, New York
JOAQUIN CASTRO, Texas
ROBIN L. KELLY, Illinois

CONTENTS

EVALUATING THE EXPORT–IMPORT BANK IN THE GLOBAL ECONOMY

FRIDAY, OCTOBER 23, 2015

House of Representatives,
Subcommittee on Terrorism, Nonproliferation, and Trade,
Committee on Foreign Affairs,
Washington, DC.

The subcommittee met, pursuant to notice, at 9:30 a.m., in room 2172, Rayburn House Office Building, Hon. Ted Poe (chairman of the subcommittee) presiding.

Mr. POE. The subcommittee will come to order. Without objection, all members may have 5 days to submit statements, questions, extraneous materials for the record subject to the length limitation in the rules.

I want to welcome all of our witnesses.

And at this time, I will give my opening statement and then yield to the ranking member Mr. Keating.

If the United States' economy wants to grow, it has to export. Ninety-five percent of a business' potential customers are not in the United States. They are in other countries. The more foreign customers we can sell American-made goods to, the more jobs we create right here in the United States.

Trade is the lifeblood of Houston in the State of Texas. Houston exports more than any other city in the United States. In Texas, more than one in five jobs are supported by trade. Fifty percent of the economy of Houston, Texas, is based on the Port of Houston. The Port of Houston is an export port. It exports all types of items throughout the world. The question for us today, does the Export-Import Bank help U.S. businesses trade and grow exports in a global economy?

Congress founded the Export-Import Bank to facilitate American trade overseas and help guarantee financing for U.S. businesses. The charter has been renewed every year since 1934. That streak of 80 years ended this year. The bank expired on July the 1st.

The concept of an export credit agency is not unique to the United States. The U.S. Ex-Im Bank is one of at least 85 export credit agencies throughout the world. Some countries have more than one. Supporters of reauthorizing Ex-Im Bank argue that eliminating the bank is tantamount to unilateral disarmament, putting U.S. companies at a competitive disadvantages with their competitors worldwide. There is no reason to believe, they say, that other counties will follow our lead to abolish their export credit agency. Instead, other countries like China and Russia will be happy to take our business for themselves.

In the last few months, we have seen that start to happen. GE announced that 100 jobs will be moved next year from a facility near my district in Houston, Texas, to Hungary and China. Why? So GE can access foreign credit export credit for its customers of gas turbines. The lapse in reauthorization impacts more than the big companies like GE. It affects many small businesses. Cindy Lewis, president of AirBorn Inc., an electronic connector manufacturer in Georgetown, Texas, put it this way: ''Maybe Boeing can weather a shutdown of the Ex-Im Bank, but small businesses in Texas that make up nearly 90 percent of transactions cannot.''

Supporters of the bank also argue that Ex-Im only finances deals that the private sector cannot finance alone. For some large infrastructure projects in international markets, the bid will not even be accepted if a company does not have access to an export credit agency.

And some billion-dollar opportunities for American companies and international markets require the availability of export credit before they will even entertain a bid. Without Ex-Im Bank to level the playing field, supporters say American companies will continue to lose out to foreign competitors backed by aggressive government support.

However, on the other hand, opponents of the bank see it as corporate welfare subsidized by taxpayer dollars. They believe the companies will be able to get the private financing needed for their business opportunities overseas. In a free market, the United States Government, opponents argue, should not pick winners and losers. While they admit that some people may lose their jobs, they also say this is a global economy and the companies moving jobs overseas, that will happen regardless of the Ex-Im Bank. They also say that this is only a minor fraction of U.S. exports being only 2 percent.

The bottom line is this: Buyers overseas want American products and no one innovates better than the United States worker. When a person combines the strength of the American spirit with a level playing field, American companies can win and can compete. The purpose of this hearing is to find out whether the unilateral eliminating of the American Ex-Im Bank has put American export industry and jobs at a global disadvantage.

And I will now yield to the ranking member from Massachusetts, Mr. Keating.

Mr. KEATING. Thank you, Chairman Poe.

And thank you for the timely and urgent hearing we are having today on the Ex-Im Bank. It is important to recognize, first of all, that the Ex-Im Bank is an independent nonpartisan agency that has helped finance the export of American goods and services for over eight decades. Not only does the agency operate at no cost to taxpayers, but it has been very prolific in sustaining 1.5 million jobs and increasing our private-sector jobs back here at home.

It produced funds each year without any participation of taxpayer funding. Yet today, partisan politics has allowed this important tool of American business interest to lapse. Since its expiration in June, our businesses and workers have been placed at a disadvantage to their international competitors and American jobs are moving overseas. This month, two major American job supporters announced that they are forced to send jobs overseas due to the Ex-Im Bank's expiration and the ongoing battle over its reauthorization.

At the very least, 500 Americans will lose their jobs and this is only the beginning. Small businesses and businesses that do exporting need certain protections to tackle the new markets and the expanding markets that are there creating the most growth in jobs in the U.S. With nearly 60 other export credit agencies around the world trying to win jobs for their own countries, Ex-Im Bank helps level the playing field for American businesses contributing to decreasing our trade deficit and encouraging exports. This agency ensures that U.S. companies do not lose out on a sale because attractive financing exists in foreign countries.

Now, I have been to the Port of Houston that the chairman has mentioned. If you just visualize the scope of that and the international commerce that is coming through that, you can see at one glance the impact of our not being able to be competitive with other countries. But you don't have to go to the Port of Houston to see that. You can go to each and every State in the United States.

One of our witnesses, Mr. Thompson, is here from my home State and he comes from Plymouth, Massachusetts. And we could have witnesses from every State in the Union here testifying today as to what the Ex-Im Bank does. In Massachusetts, the Ex-Im supported over $3 billion in exports and 22,000 jobs while on the whole, the country has had $235 billion in exports that is supported by the bank.

However, as a result of the lapse of authority on July 1, Ex-Im has halted all activities on new and pending applications. Since then, over 400 insurance policies, many of which were predominantly small businesses, have expired totaling over $490 million in that period. Once more, at the time of the lapse, more than $9 billion in transactions were sitting in the pipeline. Last May, the chairman and I held a hearing on the important role of trade and promotion agencies. We were joined by business owners and supporters from both sides of the aisle in discussing the critical role of Ex-Im and the imperative to reauthorize its role. And we were warned of the job losses and disadvantages that would result in such a lapse.

Regrettably, we are now starting to see those predictions come true. So I welcome the testimony and the insight of our witnesses today, and look forward to the conversation that will ensue. And it is my hope that today's hearing will serve as a resource for all of our colleagues who are not sold on the economic import of reauthorizing this agency. It is a critical and urgent hearing. It is timely, and I hope it produces swift results in reauthorizing the bank.

With that, I yield back, Mr. Chairman.

Mr. POE. I thank the gentleman.

The Chair will yield 1 minute to Mr. Heck from Washington for his opening statement.

Mr. HECK. Thank you very much, Mr. Chair. Might I just begin by extending my sincere appreciation to both you and the ranking member for the privilege to sit in and participate in this committee.

I am not a member of this committee. I am instead a member of the Committee on Financial Services, which is the general committee of jurisdiction for this issue and one with which I have incredible familiarity in the long effort.

I want to make just one point as it relates to the impact on the economy and businesses. Much is often made about the fact that the Boeing Company is the major user of the Export-Import Bank. Not much is made about the fact that the Boeing Company doesn't actually make airplanes. They don't. They design and assemble them. The people who actually make the airplanes are the 15,000 businesses in their supply chain, 6,000 to 8,000 of which are small businesses, and that is who will be hurt most by our failure to reauthorize the Bank.

Thank you again, Mr. Chair, very much.

Mr. POE. Mr. Castro, do you want to make an opening statement?

Mr. CASTRO. No. Please, go ahead.

Mr. POE. All right. Thank you.

The Chair will now introduce the witnesses and remind the witnesses that you have 5 minutes. We have all of your statements made part of the record. And then, after the witnesses make their comments, then members of the committee will ask questions.

Diane Katz is a senior research fellow in regulatory policy under the Institute of Economic Freedom and Opportunity at The Heritage Foundation. Prior to joining Heritage in 2010, she served as director of risk, environment, and energy policy at the Fraser Institute.

T.J. Raguso is the executive vice president and international division manager for Amegy Bank. He has 22 years of experience in trade finance, letters of credit, commercial lending, and international correspondent banking.

Tyler Schroeder is a financial analyst for Air Tractor in Texas. He works directly with Ex-Im Bank and their U.S. commercial banking partner to facilitate the sale of Air Tractor's foreign receivables and assignment of Ex-Im Bank insurance coverage.

And Dr. Loren Thompson is the chief operating officer at the Lexington Institute. He previously served as deputy director of the Security Studies Program at Georgetown University.

Welcome to all of you.

Ms. Katz, you may proceed.

STATEMENT OF MS. DIANE KATZ, SENIOR RESEARCH FELLOW IN REGULATORY POLICY, THE INSTITUTE FOR ECONOMIC FREEDOM AND OPPORTUNITY, THE HERITAGE FOUNDATION

Ms. KATZ. Thank you, Mr. Chairman, Ranking Member Keating, and members of the committee. I appreciate your invitation to testify this morning. My name is Diane Katz, and I am a senior research fellow in regulatory policy at The Heritage Foundation. The views expressed in this testimony are my own and should not be construed as representing any official position of The Heritage Foundation.

My testimony will address whether expiration of the Export-Import Bank charter is affecting U.S. trade. The short answer is no. As I detail in my written testimony, there is no shortage of private export financing, and the primary beneficiaries of Ex-Im subsidies continue to secure billions of dollars of new orders without it. For small businesses in particular, there are numerous other State and Federal programs to facilitate exporting—not that they are necessary.

Bank proponents have spent tens of millions of dollars trying to convince you that Ex-Im is a lifeline for American jobs. But export subsidies do not create or even support jobs; they simply redistribute them from unsubsidized firms to subsidized firms.

It is also important to recognize that Ex-Im finances a meager 2 percent of all U.S. exports. That means, of course, that 98 percent of exports rely on other forms of financing. And, as the chart before you illustrates, it is private financing that drives export growth.

Some Members think that the charter should be reauthorized because Ex-Im is helpful to business in their district. But helpfulness does not justify government superseding a fully functioning export finance market, particularly when the subsidies produce more harm than benefit overall. Were helpfulness the proper standard, the size and scope of government would be boundless, as it is in, say, China.

Instead, there are a great many tax and regulatory reforms that would help many more businesses to a far greater extent. As it is, the Federal Government backs an astonishing 60 percent of all financial liabilities in the U.S. The Federal Reserve Bank of Richmond, which monitors this expanding safety net, has dubbed the exercise "the bailout barometer."

In analyzing whether the charter expiration has impeded trade, we must identify the primary beneficiaries of Ex-Im programs. That turns out to be a select few multinational conglomerates. Between 2007 and 2014, more than 51 percent of Ex-Im subsidies benefited just 10 corporations. These companies—Boeing, General Electric, Bechtel, and the like—do not lack access to capital. Some even run export finance divisions of their own. And most of these industry titans also have billions of dollars of back orders that will keep them busy for years. The foreign firms that receive most Ex-Im financing are likewise corporate giants that primarily purchase products from other conglomerates, not mainstream businesses.

A tremendous amount of media attention has largely focused on the supposed travails of small businesses without Ex-Im. In actuality, Ex-Im has assisted less than ½ of 1 percent of small businesses. And even that number is overstated, as detailed in my written testimony.

The small businesses that have benefited from Ex-Im in the past can instead tap the private financing sources used by the vast majority of their brethren. Consider this: Small and medium-size businesses account for 98 percent of all exporters, and exports have reached record levels of late. Obviously, then, access to financing is not a problem. In the event a business cannot access private capital, it can still export through wholesalers or associate its operations with larger firms or global supply chains.

Notwithstanding all the fear-mongering about the loss of Ex-Im subsidies, finance costs are only one among a variety of factors that affect a purchaser's choice of supplier. Availability, reliability, and stability all play significant parts in purchase decisions. And there should be no question that American ingenuity can trump the export subsidies doled out by foreign governments.

It is, of course, understandable that Ex-Im beneficiaries want to keep their subsidies, but the impact on the rest of the economy cannot be overlooked. Because Ex-Im lowers operating costs for foreign businesses, all the American firms without subsidies suffer a competitive disadvantage in the global market.

The only way to eliminate the economic distortions and taxpayer risks of export subsidies and the rampant cronyism it perpetrates is to reject reauthorization of the Ex-Im charter.

Thank you.

[The prepared statement of Ms. Katz follows:]

The Heritage Foundation

214 Massachusetts Avenue, NE • Washington DC 20002 • (202) 546-4400 • heritage.org

CONGRESSIONAL TESTIMONY

The End of Ex-Im:
No Threat to U.S. Exports

**Testimony before
Committee on Foreign Affairs
United States House**

October 23, 2015

**Diane Katz
Senior Research Fellow in Regulatory Policy
The Heritage Foundation**

Chairman Poe, Ranking Member Keating, and Members of the Subcommittee, thank you for inviting me to testify this morning. My name is Diane Katz. I am a Senior Research Fellow in Regulatory Policy at The Heritage Foundation. The views expressed in this testimony are my own, and should not be construed as representing any official position of The Heritage Foundation.

Introduction

My testimony today will address whether the expiration of the Export-Import Bank charter has affected the ability of American companies to conduct global trade. The short answer is "No." As I document here, there is no shortage of private export financing. The primary beneficiaries of Ex-Im financing continue to secure billions of dollars of new orders without it. And, while subsidies inflict more harm than benefit, there are many state and federal programs to assist businesses—small businesses, in particular—with exporting their products and services.

A number of media outlets in recent weeks have reported that thousands of U.S. jobs are being moved overseas because Congress rejected reauthorization the Ex-Im charter. Such claims are unfounded.[1] The real story is that Boeing, General Electric and other top beneficiaries of the government bank are trying to scare Americans into further subsidizing their hugely successful multinational operations.

Bank proponents have spent tens of millions of dollars trying to convince Congress and the public that Ex-Im is a lifeline for American jobs. They also have engaged in a form of political extortion by threatening to withdraw contributions from members who do not act as they prescribe.[2] But it is critically important for Congress and the public to understand that export subsidies do not "create" or "support" jobs—they simply redistribute them from unsubsidized firms to subsidized ones. And the job numbers touted by Ex–Im advocates are dubious, at best. The Government Accountability Office, among others, has roundly criticized them as misleading.

It is likewise important to recognize that Ex-Im finances a meager 2 percent of U.S. exports. That means 98 percent of American exports (and the tens of millions of jobs that produce them) do not depend in any way on Ex-Im subsidies. Compared to other forms of financing, Ex-Im subsidies barely contribute to the growth of U.S. exports, as the chart below illustrates.

---

[1] See Diane Katz, GE's Cynical Ruse: Pretending Jobs Are Moving Because of End of Ex-Im Subsidies, Daily Signal, September 30, 2015, http://dailysignal.com/2015/09/30/ges-cynical-ruse-pretending-jobs-are-moving-because-of-end-of-ex-im-subsidies/ and Diane Katz and Veronique de Rugy, Don't buy the pro-Ex-Im hype, The Hill, September 23, 2015,, http://thehill.com/blogs/congress-blog/economy-budget/254536-dont-buy-the-pro-ex-im-hype

[2] Anna Palmer and Jeremy Herb, Boeing, GE cut off donations to Ex-Im foes, Politico.com, August 5, 2015, http://www.politico.com/story/2015/08/boeing-ge-cut-off-donations-to-ex-im-opponents-121056#ixzz3pJW9HM5i

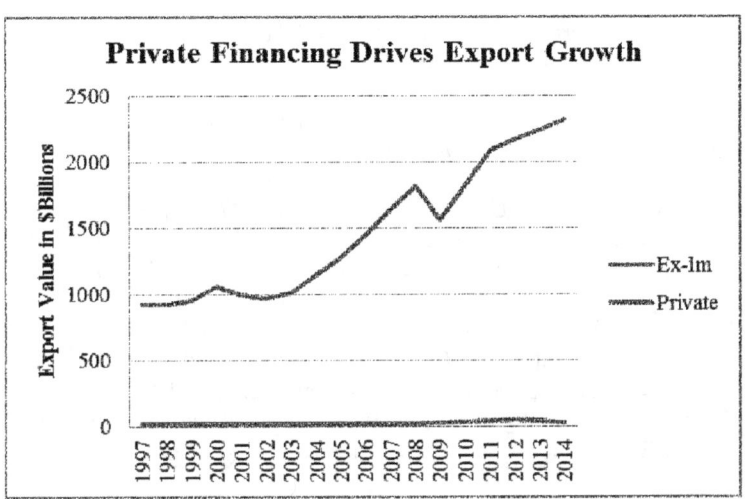

Sources: U.S. Census Bureau and annual reports of the Export-Import Bank.

Ex-Im subsidies do impose costs on taxpayers and all the American businesses without access to export subsidies. Because Ex-Im financing is effectively discounted, foreign firms that receive it enjoy artificially lower costs when purchasing goods and services. Consequently, all the unsubsidized American companies—those paying higher finance costs—are at a competitive disadvantage in the global market. Ex-Im subsidies also drive investment from unsubsidized projects to subsidized projects—regardless of the merits. That's the essence of "picking winners and losers."

Most economists agree that subsidies yield more harm than benefit. As noted by scholar Matthew Mitchell, "Whatever its guise, government-granted privilege [to private businesses] is an extraordinarily destructive force. It misdirects resources, impedes genuine economic progress, breeds corruption, and undermines the legitimacy of both the government and the private sector."[3]

It may seem understandable that lawmakers regard Ex-Im as helpful to businesses in their district. But "helpfulness" is no justification for the federal government to supersede a fully functioning export-finance market. Every government action undoubtedly helps someone, but a citizenry dependent on government favors inevitably becomes subservient. That's precisely why the Founders restricted government power—and why subsidy schemes like Ex-Im should be eliminated.

Charter Expiration and Employment
In analyzing whether the charter expiration has impeded U.S. trade, it makes sense to first identify the primary beneficiaries of Ex-Im programs. That turns out to be a select few

---

[3]Matthew Mitchell, The Pathology of Privilege: The Economic Consequences of Government Favoritism (Arlington, VA: Mercatus Center at George Mason University, 2014), 1–2, http://mercatus.org/publication/pathology-privilege-economic-consequences-government-favoritism

multinational conglomerates. Between 2007 and 2014, more than 51 percent of all Ex-Im subsidies benefitted just 10 corporations.[4]

Boeing is the biggest by far, benefitting from $66.7 billion in subsidies during the past seven years.[5] Others in the Top 10 include:

2. $8.3 billion for General Electric (market cap $279 billion)
3. $5.2 billion for Bechtel (annual revenue $32.7 billion)
4. $3.2 billion for CBI Americas Ltd. (market cap $4.4 billion)
5. $3 billion for Exxon-Mobil Corp. (market cap $337 billion)
6. $2.7 billion for Solar Turbines Inc. (a subsidiary of Caterpillar)
7. $2.3 billion for Caterpillar (market cap $42.5 billion)
8. $2.1 billion for Applied Materials Inc. (market cap $19.6 billion)
9. $2 billion for Westinghouse Electric Co. (annual sales $10 billion)
10. $1.4 billion for Noble Drilling (market cap $3.2 billion)

These and all the other deals involving titans of industry belie bank advocates' claims that Ex-Im subsidies are necessary to fill "gaps" in financing. Indeed, in the months since the charter expired, Boeing (as an example) has secured multiple export deals worth billions of dollars, including:

- An $8 billion order from Taiwan-based EVA Airways for 24 Dreamliners (787-10s) and two Extended Range jetliners (777-300ER).

- The sale of Boeing Converted Freighters (737-800) to China-based YTO Airlines.

- The sale of 22 Apache attack helicopters (AH-64E) and 15 Chinook heavy-lift helicopters (CH-47F) for the India Ministry of Defense.

- The sale of four Poseidon aircraft (P-8A) for the Royal Australian Air Force (and nine P-8As for the U.S. Navy, for a contract total of $1.49 billion).

General Electric, too, has secured multiple new orders since June 30th, including, among others:

- The sale of two high-efficiency 9HA.01 gas turbines and associated equipment for a combined-cycle power plant in Pakistan.

- The sale of advanced gas turbines for a new 3-gigawatt power plant in Iraq.

---

[4] Veronique de Rugy and Diane Katz, Export Jobs Won't Disappear Absent Ex-Im Bank, Mercatus Center at George Mason University, May 21, 2015, http://mercatus.org/publication/export-jobs-won-t-disappear-absent-ex-im-bank

[5] Veronique de Rugy, Diane Katz, and Rizqi Rachmat, "Cumulative Top Ten Ex-Im Beneficiaries, 2007–2014," Mercatus Center at George Mason University, May 20, 2015, http://mercatus.org/sites/default/files/Exim-Cumulative-Backlog-Charts.pdf

- The sale of a high-efficiency 7HA.02 gas turbine and associated clutched steam turbine (as well as a long-term services agreement) for a new combined-cycle power plant in Anyang, Korea.

- The leasing of two Boeing 777-300ER aircraft for Japan's All Nippon Airways Co., Ltd.

- A framework agreement between GE Oil & Gas and Norway's Statoil Petroleum AS for subsea operations services, including offshore installation and intervention, equipment repair and maintenance, studies, upgrades and modifications.

- The purchase of "high-end" turbomachinery for the Trans-Anatolian Natural Gas Pipeline (a partnership between the State Oil Company of Azerbaijan, Turkey's state-owned Petroleum Pipeline Corporation, and British Petroleum.

The biggest Ex-Im beneficiaries also have billions of dollars of backorders that will keep workers busy for years to come. Boeing, for example, has reported a total of 5,656 unfilled orders; General Electric has posted a backlog of $261 billion; Caterpillar Inc.'s backlog is $16.5 million (in the first quarter of 2015); and Bechtel Corp. posted a "strong" backlog of $70.5 billion.

The foreign firms that receive most Ex-Im financing are likewise large corporations that primarily purchase exports from U.S. conglomerates—not from Main Street businesses.[6] All have ready access to a variety of financing to continue their purchases of American goods and services.

---

[6]Veronique de Rugy and Diane Katz, The Export-Import Bank's Top Foreign Buyers, Mercatus Center at George Mason University, April 2015, http://mercatus.org/sites/default/files/DeRugy-Ex-Im-Foreign-Buyers.pdf

Company	Ex-Im Financing (2007-2013)	Country	Sector
Pemex-Exploracion y Producion	$7,206,653,106	Mexico	Oil & Gas
Ryanair Ltd.	$4,142,677,182	Ireland	Aviation
Emirates Airline	$3,392,703,744	United Arab Emirates	Aviation
Refineria de Cartagena S.A.	$3,215,335,836	Columbia	Oil & Gas
Esso Highlands Limited-Png Lng Project	$3,000,000,000	Papua New Guinea	Oil & Gas
Cathay Pacific Airways Ltd.	$2,952,460,537	Hong Kong	Aviation
Australia Pacific Lng Csg Processing Pty Ltd.	$2,865,507,940	Australia	Gas & Electric
Turk Hava Yotari A.O. (Turkish Airlines)	$2,538,244,371	Turkey	Aviation
Reliance Industries Ltd.	$2,400,000,000	India	Oil & Gas
National Aviation Co. of India	$2,375,441,278	India	Aviation

Five of the top 10 buyers are state-controlled and rake in millions of dollars from their own governments in addition to Ex-Im Bank subsidies. These multiple-subsidy streams offset operating costs, and thus provide a significant competitive advantage over unsubsidized U.S. firms engaged in similar ventures.

Five of the top 10 are involved in the exploration, development, and production of oil or natural gas. (These foreign concerns are collecting subsidies from American taxpayers at the same time that the Obama administration is restricting domestic oil and gas operations.[4] Consequently, the federal government has doubly disadvantaged U.S. energy firms—through its excessive regulation and Ex-Im Bank subsidies granted to foreign competitors.)

The other five top buyers are airlines that collectively have received more than $15 billion in Ex-Im subsidies in the past seven years solely to purchase products from Boeing.[5] But as noted in Boeing's latest Aircraft Finance Market Outlook, there now exists "an unprecedented diversity of capital providers."

"An expanding investor base, a rational balance between secured and unsecured funding, innovative financing structures, and a growing private placement market are helping to propel the growth of capital markets in aircraft finance."[7]

The Small Players

A tremendous amount of media attention has focused on the travails of small businesses that no longer will have access to Ex-Im subsidies. Bank proponents focus on small firms to deflect attention from the fact that the vast majority of Ex–Im beneficiaries are major corporations.

According to bank officials, about 20 percent of Ex-Im subsidies benefit small businesses. But that figure is inflated by the bank's expansive definition of "small," which includes firms with as many as 1,500 workers, as well as companies with revenues of up to $21.5 million annually.

In reality, Ex-Im assists only a tiny portion of all small businesses. Using data from the bank and the U.S. Census, economist Veronique de Rugy calculated that Ex-Im subsidies "supported" less than one-half of one percent of all small businesses.[8]

But that figure may be overstated. A recent investigation by the Reuters news agency found that potentially hundreds of the subsidy recipients categorized as "small businesses" by Ex-Im are actually very large enterprises or units of multinational conglomerates. Companies owned by billionaires such as Warren Buffet and Mexico's Carlos Slim, as well by Japanese and European conglomerates, were listed as small businesses, Reuters reported. So, too, were Austria's Swarovski jewelers, North Carolina's Global Nuclear Fuels (owned by General Electric) and Japan's Toshiba and Hitachi. The bank's list of small businesses in Texas includes engineering giant Bechtel, which has 53,000 employees.

Even the financing designed for small businesses ends up benefitting the conglomerates. Between 2007 and 2014, large corporations—rather than small businesses—collected between 19.6 and 40.1 percent of the Ex-Im Bank's working capital loans and guarantees. These included two transactions totaling $711.5 million for Boeing Co. and three transactions totaling $850 million for Ford Motor Co. (with a market cap of $58.5 billion).

The small businesses that have benefitted from Ex-Im subsidies in the past can tap the private financing sources used by the vast majority of their brethren. Given that small and medium-sized businesses account for 98 percent of all exporters, and exports have reached record levels in recent years, financing obviously is not a problem. Indeed, in an annual survey of small businesses by the National Federation of Independent Business

---

[7] Boeing Capital Corp., Current Aircraft Finance Market Outlook 2015, December 2014, http://www.boeing.com/resources/boeingdotcom/company/key_orgs/pdf/BCC-market-Report-WEB.pdf

[8] Veronique de Rugy, The Export-Import Bank Assists a Tiny Portion of All US Small Business Jobs and Firms, Mercatus Center at George Mason University, July 21, 2014, http://mercatus.org/publication/export-import-bank-assists-tiny-portion-all-us-small-business-jobs-and-firms

Research Foundation, respondents rated "Exporting My Products/Services" as the least problematic of 75 business problems.[9] (The cost of health care ranked as the most severe problem.)

Meanwhile, the number of small businesses that export (and the value of their exports) has grown significantly in recent years,[10] which belies the claim of Ex–Im proponents that small firms are unable to compete without Ex–Im financing (since the vast majority of these firms do not get such assistance). Between 1997 and 2007, for example, the value of exports per small and medium-size businesses increased by 80 percent, and the number of these exporting firms grew by 30 percent, according to the U.S. International Trade Commission. (Firms with fewer than 20 employees accounted for 95 percent of the growth.)[11]

Financing Options

Despite the fear-mongering about the outsourcing of American jobs, Congress and the public can rest assured that the consequences of charter expiration are inconsequential. Here's why:

First and foremost, as noted earlier, the vast majority of U.S. exports— 98 percent—do not receive assistance from the bank and thus have access to private financing. For those that no longer have access to Ex-Im subsidies, there is no shortage of private sources of investment. And the companies that benefit most from the subsidies— large and successful corporations such as Boeing, General Electric and Caterpillar—enjoy unparalleled access to private capital.

Second, finance costs are only one among a variety of factors that affect a purchaser's choice of supplier. Availability, reliability and stability all play significant parts in purchase decisions. There should be no question that U.S. firms are capable of competing successfully without corporate welfare.

Third, there is no such thing as a "level playing field" in trade. Every country possesses advantages that others lack. The ingenuity and drive of American enterprise can trump the export subsidies doled out by foreign governments. American companies would be further advantaged if Congress reduced the tax and regulatory barriers that inhibit business growth.

Demand for Ex–Im financing has actually declined in recent years, too. Authorizations dropped by 24 percent between FY 2012 and FY 2013, and decreased by 25 percent between FY 2013 and FY 2014.

---

[9] Holly Wade, "Small Business Problems & Priorities," National Federation of Independent Business Research Foundation, August 2012. http://www.nfib.com/Portals/0/PDF/AllUsers/research/studies/small-business-problems-priorities-2012-nfib.pdf

[10] Economic Statistics Administration, "Data Snapshot: How Much Do Small- and Medium-sized Businesses Contribute to U.S. Exports?" January 22, 2015, http://www.esa.doc.gov/under-secretary-blog/data-snapshot-how-much-do-small-and-medium-sized-businesses-contribute-us

[11] U.S. International Trade Commission, "Small and Medium-Sized Enterprises: Overview of Participation in U.S. Exports," January 2010. http://www.usitc.gov/publications/332/pub4125.pdf

Boeing's own assessment of the export finance market for aviation is very positive. According to its 2015 outlook, the company "anticipates an unprecedented diversity of capital providers," and "historically low levels of export credit usage."[12]

The report further states: "While politics are creating some uncertainty around export credit, that should be offset by balanced funding from commercial banks and capital markets. We expect to welcome a number of new commercial bank and capital market participants over the coming year, which should drive continued diversity in these sources."

In the event that a small business cannot access private capital, it can seek to export through wholesalers or associate its business operations with larger firms or with global supply chains.

Small firms can also reduce export risk by requiring upfront payment--a very common strategy among small businesses. In a 2013 survey by the National Small Business Association, 69 percent of exporters said they demand payment in advance of shipping.[13] Only 12 percent utilize any type of "payment enhancement," such as credit insurance. Nor do most small businesses lack access to private capital, as Ex–Im proponents claim: 73 percent of small businesses reported that they access export financing from a bank or credit union.

What most imperils the availability of financing are the tax and regulatory barriers erected by the government. Dodd-Frank, in particular, has increased the costs of credit. The International Chamber of Commerce reports that 70 percent of respondents to its 2015 survey say report declined transactions due to regulatory burden; a total of 91 percent expect compliance requirements to increase over the next year, up from the 81 percent in 2014."[14]

No Need for Reauthorization
It is understandable, of course, that Ex-Im beneficiaries want to keep their subsidies, but the impact on the overall economy should not be overlooked. A review of the academic literature on the topic suggests that in most cases export subsidies reduce the total income of the country paying the subsidies (i.e., the GDP of the country issuing the subsidies is negatively affected). In all cases, export subsidies reduce worldwide income by increasing the wealth of those, and only those, who are subsidized—at the expense of other exporters and taxpayers.[15]

---

[12] Boeing Capital Corp., Current Aircraft Finance Market Outlook 2015, December 2014, http://www.boeing.com/resources/boeingdotcom/company/key_orgs/pdf/BCC-market-Report-WEB.pdf

[13] National Small Business Association and Small Business Exporters Association, "2013 Small Business Exporting Survey," http://www.nsba.biz/wp-content/uploads/2013/06/Exporting-Survey-2013.pdf

[14] International Chamber of Commerce, Global Survey on Trade Finance, September 29, 2015, http://www.iccwbo.org/Products-and-Services/Trade-facilitation/ICC-Global-Survey-on-Trade-Finance/

[15] Salim Furth, "The Export Import Bank: What The Scholarship Says." (Backgrounder No. 2934, Heritage Foundation, Washington, DC, August 7, 2014), http://www.heritage.org/research/reports/2014/08/the-export-import-bank-what-the-scholarship-says

This was further documented by economist Dan Ikenson in a 2014 study in which he quantified the industrial "winners" and "victims" of Ex-Im subsidies. Not surprisingly, Ikenson found that Ex-Im policies benefit far fewer industries than they penalize: Out of 236 manufacturing industries studied, 189 are victims, incurring a combined annual net cost of almost $3 billion.

Ikenson's study did not account for the costs imposed on domestic manufacturers who compete with Ex-Im–subsidized domestic exporters, nor did it consider what alternative opportunities might have been otherwise viable in the absence of subsidies. If these indirect costs are factored in, the total true costs of Ex-Im subsidies would likely be greater.[16]

Even if Ex-Im subsidies were actually helpful and less harmful, government interference in business finance has become unsustainable. According to the "Bailout Barometer" developed by the Federal Reserve Bank of Richmond, a whopping 60 percent of all liabilities of the financial system are explicitly or implicitly protected from loss by the federal government—i.e., taxpayers.[17]

This federal "safety net" undermines the financial discipline that is so necessary for the free enterprise system to properly function. Absent government "protection," investors only take risks they are able to manage. But a bailout mechanism encourages excessive risk-taking because investors do not bear the cost of their actions. All of which increases the likelihood of financial crises and bailouts.

Conclusion

Despite overwhelming evidence to the contrary, some members of Congress believe that a few legislative tweaks will remedy all that is wrong with the Export-Import Bank (Ex-Im). But Ex-Im has failed to fully comply with previous reforms mandated by Congress.

Lawmakers would do well to consider the many drawbacks of the subsidies, including distortions in the distribution of labor and capital, higher consumer costs, and the disadvantages to domestic firms that do not receive the subsidies. Moreover, there has been a recent uptick in allegations of serious misconduct by Ex-Im Bank employees. The Office of Inspector General has identified deficiencies in internal controls that reduce the reliability of the bank to ferret out improper payments. There also are weaknesses in the bank's "Character, Reputational, Transactional Integrity" screening of applicants, as well as a pattern of insufficient due diligence by delegated lenders, specifically lenders with a history of defaulted transactions.

---

[16]Daniel J. Ikenson, The Export-Import Bank and Its Victims: Which Industries and States Bear the Brunt?, Cato Institute Policy Analysis No. 756, September 10, 2014, http://www.cato.org/publications/policy-analysis/export-import-bank-its-victims-which-industries-states-bear-brunt

[17]Federal Reserve Bank of Richmond, Bailout Barometer: How Large is the Financial Safety Net?, May 13, 2015, https://www.richmondfed.org/safetynet/

In fact, pending legislation is largely a regurgitation of "reforms" previously mandated by Congress—without appreciable effect. The only meaningful way to remedy Ex-Im's multibillion-dollar risk to taxpayers—and the rampant cronyism the export subsidies perpetrate—is to reject reauthorization of the charter.

Mr. POE. Thank you, Ms. Katz.

Mr. Raguso, you have 5 minutes.

STATEMENT OF MR. T.J. RAGUSO, EXECUTIVE VICE PRESIDENT, INTERNATIONAL DIVISION, AMEGY BANK NATIONAL ASSOCIATION

Mr. RAGUSO. Chairman Poe, Ranking Member Keating, and members of the subcommittee, thank you for the opportunity to appear before you this morning.

Amegy Bank is a commercial bank with offices in Houston, Dallas, and San Antonio. We are primarily a commercial lender, which is to say we are especially focused on lending to businesses. We have more than 40,000 commercial customers in Texas, many of which are small businesses.

As a bank with a regional focus, we make loans that reflect the markets we serve. We have a strong energy focus, but our lending supports many industries, including manufacturing and service.

Trade is important to our bank, as Texas has been the largest exporting State for the last 12 years and accounts for roughly 12 percent of U.S. exports. Amegy Bank has a significant presence in Houston, the largest exporting city in the U.S. Simply put, when you are a bank, you play with the cards you are dealt. In Texas, that means international business.

Amegy Bank has used Ex-Im programs for over 20 years. Last year, Amegy Bank authorized more than $100 million in Ex-Im-guaranteed loans in Texas, 60 percent of which were to small businesses.

Exporting provides revenue diversification to our customers and to the economy. This is especially true when conditions are weak in the domestic market, as they are now. As we saw in the last downturn, Ex-Im utilization increases when the economy is in recession. We see an increased need now, given the impact of lower commodity prices and reduced global trade.

Access to commercial bank borrowing is critical to a company's competitiveness. However, lending to an exporting company presents additional risks. Some of these risks include foreign receivables, geopolitical risk, unfamiliar legal system, and longer delivery or payment terms.

Amegy Bank uses the Ex-Im Working Capital Guarantee Program to mitigate these risks because bank credit policies require a conservative view of international risk and restrict borrowing against export-related collateral. This means less money to our customers to finance their businesses. There is no equivalent private-sector alternative for this program. Ex-Im complements, rather than competes, with Amegy Bank.

CECA Supply and Services, an oil field equipment exporter focused on the Algerian market, is an example of an Amegy Bank customer whose success depends on Ex-Im Bank. CECA encouraged me to share their story with the committee today.

CECA exports 100 percent of its product and benefits from both an Ex-Im working capital loan as well as Ex-Im insurance. Over the last 9 years, CECA's revenues and export financing levels have more than tripled. Ex-Im programs have directly supported this growth. The words of CECA's CEO, Maher Touma, explain it best:

''For us, it is not a cheaper source of financing. We are either in business or we are not. For us, it is the only financing option.''

No Ex-Im programs would lead to direct job loss at CECA and possibly its suppliers and logistics suppliers. These indirect exporters contribute to exports by supplying and supporting larger companies that are the ultimate exporters.

Charter expiration negatively impacts both Amegy Bank and its customers. Most importantly, we cannot approve new deals or modify existing ones. One customer has a $33 million contract opportunity, but no viable private-sector solution has been found.

Charter expiration makes long-term planning difficult. Uncertain about the availability and the cost of financing has made some customers reluctant to bid on new projects. Our customers invest years in developing international markets, so the effects of the recent uncertainly and charter lapse may be felt for years to come.

Our customers already report increased competition supported by foreign export credit agencies, especially the Chinese. China's ECAs have financed more in the last 2 years than Ex-Im has in its entire 81-year history.

The future of Amegy's existing Ex-Im loan portfolio is uncertain. Current deals remain in effect until maturity, when they must be repaid or refinanced through other sources. Given the lack of private-sector alternatives, Amegy will look at each transaction to evaluate options, which will likely result in less financing available and increased cost.

In conclusion, Amegy Bank uses Ex-Im programs to support Main Street businesses, and the loans approved by Amegy Bank have supported the creation of hundreds of jobs. We have never experienced a loss on an Ex-Im working capital loan, and our customers have paid over $8 million in Ex-Im guarantee fees over the last 18 years.

Our customers need Ex-Im and have no confidence that global trade policy or unilateral disarmament will level the playing field. They are primarily concerned with winning the next deal, investing in their businesses, making payroll, and beating foreign competitors. No Ex-Im means fewer financing options, higher costs, and decreased competitiveness.

The future of Ex-Im Bank matters to my bank because it matters to our customers. Thank you for allowing me the opportunity to present our views on this important subject.

[The prepared statement of Mr. Raguso follows:]

TESTIMONY OF

THOMAS J. RAGUSO

EXECUTIVE VICE PRESIDENT

AMEGY BANK N.A.

Before the

COMMITTEE ON FOREIGN AFFAIRS
SUBCOMMITTEE ON TERRORISM NON-PROLIFERATION AND TRADE

UNITED STATES HOUSE OF REPRESENTATIVES

Subcommittee Hearing: Evaluating the Export-Import Bank in the Global Economy

October 23, 2015

I. Introduction

Chairman Poe, Ranking Member Keating, and members of the Subcommittee, thank you for the opportunity to appear before you this morning. I am Executive Vice President of International Banking at Amegy Bank N.A., a commercial bank with offices in Houston, Dallas and San Antonio. We are primarily a commercial lender, which is to say that we are especially focused on lending to businesses. We have more than 40,000 commercial customers in Texas, many of which are small businesses.

As a bank with a regional focus, we make loans that reflect the markets we serve. We have a strong energy focus, but our lending supports many industries including manufacturing and service. Trade is important to our bank as Texas has been the largest exporting state for the last 12 years and accounts for roughly 12% of U.S. exports. Amegy Bank has a significant presence in Houston, the largest exporting city in the U.S. Simply put, when you are a bank you play with the cards you are dealt. In Texas that means international business.

Amegy Bank has used Ex-Im programs for over 20 years. Last year, Amegy Bank authorized more than $100 million in Ex-Im guaranteed loans in Texas, 60% of which were to small businesses[1].

II. The Need for Export Financing

Exporting provides revenue diversification to our customers and the economy. This is especially true when conditions are weak in the domestic market as they are now. As we saw in the last downturn, Ex-Im utilization increases when the economy is in recession. We see an increased need now given the impact of lower commodity prices and reduced global trade. Access to commercial bank borrowing is critical to a company's competitiveness; however, lending to an exporting company presents additional risks. Some of these risks include foreign receivables, geopolitical risk, unfamiliar legal system, and longer delivery or payment terms. Amegy Bank uses the Ex-Im Working Capital Guarantee Program[2] to mitigate these risks because bank credit policies require a conservative view of international risk and restrict borrowing against export-related collateral (primarily foreign receivables and inventory). This means less

---

[1] In 2014 Amegy Bank was named Ex-Im Bank Small Business Lender of the Year and has supported transactions as small as $200,000.

[2] The Ex-Im Working Capital Guarantee program provides a 90% guarantee to lenders and is a way for banks to share risk with Ex-Im. Ex-Im charges a guarantee fee to compensate for the risk, much in the way that banks charge interest, or as insurance companies charge premiums to underwrite a risk.

money to our customers to finance their businesses. There is no equivalent private sector alternative for this program. Ex-Im complements, rather than competes with Amegy Bank.

III. Ex-Im Transaction Example[3]

CECA Supply and Services Inc., an oilfield equipment exporter focused on the Algerian market, is an example of an Amegy Bank customer whose success depends on Ex-Im Bank. CECA encouraged me to share their story with the subcommittee today. CECA exports 100% of its product and benefits from both an Ex-Im Working Capital loan as well as Ex-Im insurance. Over the last nine years, CECA's revenues and export financing needs have more than tripled. Ex-Im programs have directly supported this growth. The words of CECA CEO Maher Touma explain it best - "For us, it's not a cheaper source of financing. We're either in business or we're not. For us it's the only financing option." No Ex-Im programs would lead to direct job loss at CECA, and possibly its suppliers and logistics providers. These "Indirect Exporters[4]," contribute to exports by supplying and supporting larger companies that are the ultimate exporters.

IV. Impacts of Charter Expiration

Charter expiration negatively impacts both Amegy Bank and its customers. Most importantly, we cannot approve new deals or modify existing ones. One customer has a $33 million contract opportunity, but no viable private sector solution has been found. Charter expiration makes long-term planning difficult. Uncertainty about the availability and cost of financing has made some customers reluctant to bid on new projects. Our customers invest years in developing international markets, so the effects of the recent uncertainty and charter lapse may be felt for years to come. Our customers already report increased competition supported by foreign export credit agencies, especially the Chinese. China's ECAs have financed more in the last two years than Ex-Im has in its entire 81-year history.

The future of Amegy's existing Ex-Im loan portfolio is uncertain. Current deals remain in effect until maturity, when they must be repaid or refinanced through other sources. Given the lack of private sector alternatives, Amegy will look at each transaction to evaluate options, which will likely result in less financing available and increased cost.

---

[3] See Exhibit I for transaction examples. Amegy client Ex-Im testimonials can be found at https://www.amegybank.com/landing-pages/ex-im/cid=em_102015.

[4] Certain indirect exporters are eligible for Ex-Im support.

V. Conclusion

Amegy Bank uses Ex-Im programs to support Main Street businesses and the loans approved by Amegy Bank have supported the creation of hundreds of jobs. We have never experienced a loss on an Ex-Im working capital loan and our customers have paid over $8 million in Ex-Im guarantee fees over the last 18 years. Our customers need Ex-Im and have no confidence that global trade policy or unilateral disarmament will level the playing field. They are primarily concerned with winning the next export deal, investing in their businesses, making payroll, and beating foreign competitors. No Ex-Im means fewer financing options, higher costs and decreased competitiveness. The future of Ex-Im Bank matters to my bank because it matters to our customers. Thank you for allowing me the opportunity to present our institution's views on this important subject.

EXHIBIT I

Following are advantages that the Ex-Im Working Capital Program offers to exporters and to the U.S. economy that may not be feasible in the private sector, along with examples of Amegy Bank's Ex-Im customers and transactions that have benefitted from these advantages.

Amegy client Ex-Im testimonials can be found at https://www.amegybank.com/landing-pages/ex-im?cid=cm_102015.

- **Ex-Im Bank requires exports to contain a minimum amount of U.S. content, meaning the exports must consist of components made in the U.S. and services must be provided by U.S. personnel that meet the minimum requirements. By directly supporting one company, Ex-Im Bank loans support multiple U.S. companies and jobs in the supply chain.**

Amegy Bank's customer is a small manufacturer of specialized equipment sold primarily into the refining industry. The company is a supplier to a large engineering company and therefore an indirect exporter to the Reficar Refinery project in Colombia, which is supported by Ex-Im long-term financing. As an indirect exporter, the company is required to complete an exporter's certificate confirming that its products meet the minimum U.S. content requirement. Although cheaper foreign substitutes are available, the customer sources more expensive U.S. components to meet Ex-Im U.S. content requirements.

- **As a source of working capital, Ex-Im Bank helps exporters compete in the global marketplace**

Amegy Bank's customer is a small independent consulting company that provides engineering services focusing on oil and gas. The company's primary challenge is cash requirements to grow internationally. Foreign taxes, accounting practices, and invoicing guidelines make for slow payments from foreign buyers, and the company cannot function without the cash availability from the Ex-Im supported loan. Because of the working capital loan supported by Ex-Im over the last five years, the company has been able to double its revenues. If Ex-Im support becomes unavailable, the company will be forced to seek alternate financing with foreign banks.

- **There is a demand for Ex-Im Bank support and businesses are willing to pay for it.**

Amegy Bank's customer is manufacturer of specialized components for extracting oil and gas. When the company first became a user of Ex-Im supported financing in 2014, it experienced sticker shock at the Ex-Im guarantee fee. Soon afterwards, oil prices fell. This led to a significant reduction in the company's domestic contracts which would have resulted in job cuts, essentially putting the company in survival mode, were it not for the Ex-Im loan. The Ex-Im loan allowed the company to receive and fulfill larger international contracts. The company felt the benefits of the Ex-Im loan firsthand, and when the annual guarantee fee became due upon renewal, the company knew that the Ex-Im loan was well worth the cost.

- **Ex-Im is able to provide inventory financing to manufacturers which is available on a very limited basis on a traditional commercial loan.**

Amegy Bank's customer is a manufacturer of maritime equipment whose main competitor is a large global company. The company's manufacturing period is up to 36 months, and therefore requires bank support. Ex-Im Bank loans offer a structure that allows the company to be awarded millions of dollars' worth of international contracts. Without Ex-Im support, as a small business, the company would not be able to obtain the financing necessary to manufacture its products and would lose international business to its foreign competitor.

- **Without Ex-Im Bank support and viable private sector alternatives, U.S. companies will lose contracts to foreign competitors.**

Amegy Bank's customer is a small business that manufactures control systems for power plants. It began its relationship at Amegy Bank in 2006 with an Ex-Im loan. Over the last nine years, its revenues have increased almost 100 times due to international expansion, and it has created 40 full time jobs that would not have been possible without the Ex-Im Bank loan. The company currently has an opportunity for a contract in Sub-Saharan Africa that will come to fruition only if Ex-Im Bank is reauthorized and support is available; there is no viable plan B and the opportunity (that has been developed for years) will be lost to foreign competitors.

- **When private sector support is not available, Ex-Im supports small businesses, and contributes to their growth and success.**

Amegy Bank's customer specializes in reservoir management consulting. In 2010, it was small business with 15 employees and the majority of its contracts were export-related averaging $5 million. Prior to approaching Amegy Bank, the company had visited six other banks and none of them were willing to support its international sales. Amegy introduced the company to the Ex-Im Working Capital Guarantee Program, which allowed the company to grow into a large business, increasing revenues ten times over in a five year period. Headcount increased to 108 (full time and contract) giving the company the ability to accept contracts ranging from $250,000 to $100 million and above.

- **Long-standing businesses that have historically been able to self-finance can be affected by local economic/industry conditions and require financing to support international sales**

Amegy Bank's customer is a manufacturer of oilfield service tools. Although the company had both domestic and international sales, it did not require financing for many years. After 2007-08 economic downturn, the company saw a reduction in domestic sales and an increase in foreign sales, generating a need for export financing. Ex-Im supported financing has allowed the company to grow its international sales, making 2014 the best year ever in the company's 100 year history.

Mr. Poe. Mr. Schroeder?

STATEMENT OF MR. TYLER SCHROEDER, FINANCIAL ANALYST, AIR TRACTOR INC.

Mr. Schroeder. Good morning. Chairman Poe, Ranking Member Keating, members of the committee, I thank you for allowing me the opportunity to be here today to provide testimony on behalf of the 270 employee owners of Air Tractor, Incorporated. Today I am going to tell you the wide-ranging benefits that the Export-Import Bank has had on our businesses and to thousands of small businesses across the country.

My name is Tyler Schroeder. I am a financial analyst at Olney-based Air Tractor. Mr. Poe, you have been in Abilene for some time; you probably know where Olney is. But for the rest of you who don't know, Olney is the epitome of the middle of nowhere. We are 100 miles west of Fort Worth, and we are 200 miles east of Lubbock.

Air Tractor is a small business manufacturing firefighting and agricultural airplanes, more commonly known as crop dusters. We were founded in 1972 by a gentleman named Leland Snow. We are a small business. We have 270 employees, and, since 2007, we have been 100-percent employee-owned.

Like most small businesses in the country, we began by selling, producing, and marketing our product mainly to the domestic market. Up until 1995, we only exported 10 percent of our sales each year. Those were only facilitated through the requirement of cash in advance or an acceptable letter of credit.

It was in the mid-1990s that Air Tractor began to realize that our domestic market was becoming saturated and that for the future growth of Air Tractor the only option was to go overseas. We also realized at this time that the requirement of cash in advance was not an acceptable method to grow our export portfolio. We had to be able to compete on financing in country.

Naturally, with little expertise in the global export finance arena, we turned to our U.S. banking sector, to quickly find that no one was willing or able to give medium-term credit to our foreign small-business purchasers.

It was shortly after this that we were eventually led to the Medium-Term Credit Insurance Program at the Export-Import Bank of the United States. Through this Medium-Term Credit Insurance Program, Air Tractor is able to extend 5- to 7-year medium-term financing, normally in the form of a 5- to 7-year promissory note, whereas we purchase an insurance policy from the Export-Import Bank and attach it to this particular promissory note to defend us in the event of a default or economic risk.

What this also does is allows us to quickly turn around and liquefy that paper by selling it to our U.S. commercial bank for cash. Air Tractor is a small business. We are not a bank. We do not have the capacity on our balance sheet to extend 5- to 7-year terms and then withhold that paper for the long term.

We have been using the Medium-Term Credit Insurance Program at Export-Import Bank for over 20 years now. In the meantime, we have completed 200-plus transactions in the medium-term program, and, to this day, we have never filed a medium-term insurance claim with the Ex-Im Bank.

What we have done, though, is we have increased our exports from 10 percent in the mid-1990s to 50 percent annually today. We have also increased our employment base, from 120 employees in 1995 to 270 today. We have over doubled our production.

However, since the charter lapsed in June, Air Tractor has felt the pain. It comes at a time when our largest exporting market of Brazil is facing its own economic constraints. The Brazilian real is depreciating, the U.S. dollar is appreciating, and it is becoming more and more expensive to purchase a U.S.-based Air Tractor aircraft.

At the time that the Bank lapsed, we had 16 airplanes that were destined for our South American emerging markets, and they all required Ex-Im Bank financing. When the charter lapsed, Air Tractor scrambled to put a short-term patch together that included the private insurance sector. It was really to no avail. Of those 16 aircraft, thus far we have only been able to finalize the sale and export of 6 of those aircraft. Make no mistake that there is no alternative in the private sector for what Ex-Im Bank provides Air Tractor.

I have sat here and I have told you who Air Tractor is, how we are impacted by Ex-Im Bank, how it has helped us succeed. I would like to tell you a few things that Air Tractor is not. Air Tractor is not a deep-pocketed investor trying to push our own political agenda. Air Tractor is not a lobbying firm. We don't have a team of lobbyists up here for us talking to you guys. We do this on our own dime, on our own time.

Air Tractor is a small business in a very small town of 3,000 people who has been able to create jobs through exports. Nobody sees Olney, Texas, as a place that that happens, but indeed it does. It does. It is in small-town America. We can do this. And Ex-Im Bank is the tool that allows us to do this. Please, let us continue to do that.

Thank you.

[The prepared statement of Mr. Schroeder follows:]

Testimony of Tyler Schroeder
Financial Analyst
Air Tractor, Inc.

House Foreign Affairs Subcommittee on Terrorism,
Nonproliferation, and Trade

Hearing:
"Evaluating the Export-Import Bank in the Global Economy"

October 23, 2015

2170 Rayburn House Office Building
Washington, DC 20515

Chairman Poe, Ranking Member Keating, and members of the subcommittee, thank you for the invitation and opportunity to testify on the reauthorization of the Export-Import Bank of the United States ("Ex-Im"). My name is Tyler Schroeder, and I am a financial analyst at Air Tractor, Inc. ("Air Tractor") of Olney, Texas.

It is my privilege to submit the following testimony on behalf of the 270 employee owners of Air Tractor to the Foreign Affairs Subcommittee on Terrorism, Nonproliferation, and Trade for the hearing entitled "Evaluating the Export-Import Bank in the Global Economy." Air Tractor thanks you for holding this hearing on such a vitally important institution to thousands of exporting businesses across the country. I am honored by the invitation and opportunity to attest to the wide ranging benefits the Export-Import Bank ("Ex-Im") provides to American businesses competing abroad, as well as the implications of the current lapse in Ex-Im's authority. In this testimony, I will first provide a brief introduction of Air Tractor, an insight into Ex-Im's role in Air Tractor's growth and success, and then a glimpse into the negative implications Ex-Im's lapse in authority has had, and will continue to have on Air Tractor and similar businesses.

Introduction into Air Tractor

Air Tractor is a small business engaged in the manufacturing of agricultural and forestry fire-fighting aircraft. We are a small business of 270 employees and are 100% employee owned. Air Tractor began manufacturing specialized agricultural aircraft (crop dusters) in 1972 and is still solely located in the small rural Texas town of Olney. Olney is located 100 miles west of Fort Worth, Texas and 200 miles east of Lubbock, Texas with a population of merely 3,000 people.

Air Tractor began using the services of Ex-Im in 1995 to foster growth in our export sales portfolio. Up until this time, exports comprised approximately ten percent of total new airplane sales annually. These exports were entirely facilitated with the requirement of cash in advance or acceptable letter of credit from our end user customer. During this time, it was becoming clear that our domestic market was saturated and that the future growth of Air Tractor must come from our ability to export more competitively. We realized very quickly that to have any amount of success increasing our exports, Air Tractor needed the ability to offer credit terms to foreign purchasers.

Ex-Im's Role in the Success and Growth of Air Tractor

With little expertise in the global export finance arena, we were guided to Ex-Im's Medium Term Credit Insurance program. Through this program, Air Tractor was able to extend credit to our customers in foreign countries for the purchase of our aircraft. This credit extension takes the form of a promissory note payable to Air Tractor from our end user customer. The terms of these notes range from 5 to 7 years (medium term), and are usually payable in equal semi-annual installments with accrued interest. After a strict credit evaluation of our customer in question, Air Tractor will submit a credit application to Ex-Im Bank for their underwriting. Upon their credit approval, Ex-Im issues a Medium Term Credit Insurance policy in favor of that particular customer. Once this policy is in place, Air Tractor then has the ability to sell that note to our U.S. commercial bank for cash. As a small business, Air Tractor does not have the capacity on our balance sheet to extend and hold medium term paper of that significance. It is only with credit insurance that our U.S. commercial bank is willing and able to convert our outstanding notes to cash.

Air Tractor completed our first Ex-Im supported transaction in 1995 through the sale of two fire-fighting aircraft to a customer in Spain who was unable to establish credit in country. The transaction and payment was carried out flawlessly, and since that time, Air Tractor has sold nearly ninety aircraft in Spain without the need for Ex-Im credit insurance. Ex-Im allowed Air Tractor to gain a foothold in that market, giving the banking sector in Spain time to develop an appetite for medium term credit.

In our largest export market of Brazil, Air Tractor faces stiff competition from a local manufacturer (Embraer) of agricultural aircraft. These aircraft are heavily subsidized by the Brazilian government through the Brazilian Export Credit Agency known as BNDES. While Ex-Im is unable to offer similar terms given by BNDES, it has afforded Air Tractor the ability to offer terms close enough to compete on product quality rather than financing alone. With Ex-Im Bank's assistance, Air Tractor has increased our share of total new sales into Brazil for the past several years.

Air Tractor has now used Ex-Im's Medium Term Credit Insurance program for over twenty years. We have completed in excess of 200 export transactions, and to this day have never made a single claim on a medium term insured note – a testament to the strict underwriting standards of Ex-Im Bank. In that time Air Tractor has increased our total export sales from 10% in 1995 to approximately 50% annually and increased our employment base from 120 to 270 full time employees. Ex-Im has helped create jobs in the rural town of Olney, Texas.

As Air Tractor grows and succeeds overseas, so does our supply chain of hundreds of small businesses, many of them family owned "Mom and Pop" shops. Dietzel Aerospace is a family owned business in Kerrville, TX that supplies fiberglass hopper tanks on each and every aircraft Air Tractor produces. Dietzel Aerospace has 6 full time employees, the majority of which are family members, and counts on Air Tractor for 99.5% of their annual revenue. A retraction in Air Tractor's business of any magnitude has exponential effects on a small business like Dietzel Aerospace.

Air Tractor's use of Ex-Im insurance has also been a winning formula for the U.S. taxpayer. As a financial service provider, Ex-Im charges fees for the use of its products and services, and Air Tractor has gladly paid those fees. In the period from FY2011 to FY2014, Air Tractor paid US$4,843,430.67 to Ex-Im Bank for participating in their Medium Term Insurance program. This amount has helped Ex-Im Bank return excess funds to the U.S. Treasury for decades – a rare self-sustaining government agency which actually makes money for the U.S. taxpayer.

Implications of Ex-Im's Lapse in Authority

Ex-Im's congressional authorization to approve new funding and export insurance lapsed on June 30, 2015 and Air Tractor has felt its impact. For example, in FY2014, Air Tractor exported 76 aircraft – 52% of our total sales during that year. Through the third quarter of FY2015, as Air Tractor is exiting our heavy export season, we have exported a total of 35 aircraft – 31% of total aircraft on our production schedule for FY2015. Air Tractor was able to complete only two aircraft exports using Ex-Im Medium Term Credit Insurance before authorization lapsed, leaving the bulk of our export transactions without needed financial support from Ex-Im.

South America has been Air Tractor's largest export market for many years, as well as our largest need for Ex-Im financing facilitation. While this area of emerging markets has a high perceived risk, it is the source of Air Tractor's largest market growth in the past fifteen years. At the time Ex-Im's authorization lapsed, Air Tractor had 16 aircraft destined for South American buyers and Ex-Im medium term insurance support. In an effort to maintain our current market momentum and to finalize the sale to many of these customers with outstanding production deposits, Air Tractor struggled to create a temporary medium term funding solution.

In order to ensure our ability to liquefy export receivables, Air Tractor pursued medium term insurance through private sector firms. While this would allow us to convert paper in the U.S. commercial banking sector, the solution proved very restrictive on Air Tractor and our South American customers, resulting in several aircraft left in Air Tractor's hangars and no sale being made. These unfavorable factors include the following:

- Private sector insurance has been unwilling to extend beyond 5 year terms to our largest South American markets that are currently demanding 7 year financing
- Private sector insurance does not provide 100% coverage on collateralized transactions
- With a different pricing structure, Air Tractor has been forced to drastically reduce the coverage sought in order to maintain our customers appetite for the sale
- Private insurance policies are written to include significant first loss deductibles which are restrictive to small businesses
- Private insurance companies have historically had an inconsistent presence in many of Air Tractor's markets
- Air Tractor's commercial banking partner must first approve the credit of any private insurance company we may use

The above disproves the notion that the private sector has the ability or willingness to fill any gap left by Ex-Im's lapse in authorization. Of the 16 aircraft that were left without Ex-Im support, we have thus far been able to finalize the sale of only 6 aircraft. The remaining 10 aircraft were produced for buyers who either have delayed their purchase seeking alternative means, or have cancelled their purchase entirely because of the political uncertainty surrounding the bank.

This private sector solution does not provide a viable alternative to Ex-Im Bank support in the long term. Air Tractor will not have the ability to restrict such significant capital on an annual basis much beyond this year. Aircraft manufacturing is a capital intensive industry with large lead times and offsetting cash flow, and Air Tractor operates with this cash flow. Any restrictions on our capital will result in a shrinkage of aircraft produced, a stoppage of all future expansion, and potentially a shrinkage in our employee base. Air Tractor views our export markets as future high growth areas. South America is a vital producer of protein for a growing global middle class, and Sub-Saharan Africa has the available arable land to help feed a global population that is projected to reach 9.5 billion in the next three decades. These areas require agricultural aircraft, and Air Tractor has the opportunity to meet that requirement if we can maintain the ability to offer competitive credit. Ex-Im Bank is in Air Tractor's plan for future growth. A lack of Ex-Im Bank drastically reduces Air Tractor's plans for future job creation. Air Tractor has no solution for the continued lack of Ex-Im Bank authorization.

Approximately twenty-five percent of Air Tractor's new aircraft sales require Ex-Im Bank Medium Term Credit Insurance and are immediately at risk with the continued lapse in Ex-Im's authority. This translates into twenty-five percent of our workforce being immediately at risk, or 68 jobs. In a community of 3,000 residents, this will have a real impact on the lives supported by Air Tractor, and the Olney, Texas businesses supported by the individuals we employ.

We believe Air Tractor's situation to be a microcosm for other small businesses across this country. Many people do not think of economic growth in exporting and manufacturing originating in the small rural community of Olney, TX, but that's what Ex-Im Bank has allowed. When Air Tractor had a desire to export twenty years ago, Ex-Im proved to be the only institution willing to work with us. Ex-Im is mandated to allocate 20% of its funding for small businesses, and more importantly, routinely approves 90% of its transactions in favor of small business as defined by the U.S. Small Business Administration. Ex-Im Bank supported more than 3,340 transactions for small businesses in FY2014, even with the negative political landscape surrounding the bank during this time.

Air Tractor's future growth is undoubtedly through our ability to export aircraft, and we believe this to be true for the U.S. economy. Lacking the export services of Ex-Im Bank will be disastrous on our company and the employees and families we support. Air Tractor has demonstrated the ability to create and sustain jobs in the smallest and most rural communities. It can be done; it is being done; it needs to be done. Ex-Im Bank is a tool that allows us to make job creation a reality.

On behalf of the 270 employee owners of Air Tractor in Olney, Texas, I urge you all to take quick action on the part of Congress on a long-term reauthorization of Ex-Im Bank.

I thank Chairman Poe and Ranking Member Keating for holding this hearing, and for allowing me the opportunity to testify.

———————

Mr. POE. Thank you, Mr. Schroeder.
Dr. Thompson?

STATEMENT OF LOREN B. THOMPSON, PH.D., CHIEF OPERATING OFFICER, LEXINGTON INSTITUTE

Mr. THOMPSON. Thank you for the opportunity to be here today.

I have been asked to assess the consequences of failing to reauthorize the Ex-Im Bank, which, as you noted in your opening remarks, has been a significant contributor to U.S. trade competitiveness for eight decades. The Bank's authority to extend new credit only lapsed 4 months ago, so it is a bit early to assess all the fallout. My statement will focus on consequences that can be confidently predicted in the years ahead if no reauthorization occurs and, therefore, the Bank has to wind down its programs.

Near as I can tell, there will be no positive consequences, no gains to the United States from losing Ex-Im. Taxpayers won't save any money because Ex-Im already pays for itself. The government won't get smaller because other steps will need to be taken in order to level the playing field for U.S. exports. And the economy won't become more competitive because it will operate at a disadvantage with countries that still offer export credit.

So the consequences of shutting down the Export-Import Bank are negative for pretty much everybody, except perhaps our trade rivals. I will therefore devote the balance of my remarks to what America will lose if Ex-Im permanently ceases operations.

First, we will lose American's sole export credit agency. Every major trading nation has a government agency dedicated to mitigating risk and facilitating finance in international trade. America would be the only big industrial country without such an agency, leaving its exporters dependent on private lenders who have already stated that they will not fill the vacuum created by Ex-Im's demise.

Second, we will lose global market share in key industries. Many overseas buyers require government guarantees as a condition of bidding, which U.S. exporters could no longer secure. Even if such guarantees were not required, foreign customers would find it easier to obtain financing on favorable terms from countries with export credit agencies, so that is where they would go for their jet liners, for their earth movers, for their locomotives.

Third, we will lose more ground in the U.S. trade balance at a time when America's non-petroleum trade balance is already the worst on record. The tidal wave of foreign goods reaching these shores has reduced our growth rate by a full percentage point in recent quarters. In other words, instead of having 2.6, we could have had 3.6. But allowing Ex-Im to die would make that problem even worse.

Fourth, we will lose tens of thousands of jobs if companies like Boeing and General Electric—and, by the way, Boeing is not a multinational conglomerate. It sources 80 percent of its content in the United States. We will see Boeing and GE, the big companies, have to move overseas in order to remain competitive. Hundreds of small companies will simply cease exporting.

Initially, the job losses would come within the companies and among their suppliers. But there will be additional job losses because all the money that export workers spent on groceries, on teachers, on policemen, on dry cleaners in their communities, that will be reduced, and so there will be ripple effects.

Fifth, we will lose even more of America's domestic manufacturing base, which once was said to be the arsenal of democracy but now has shrunk to barely 12 percent of our economy. It simply isn't feasible anymore for big manufacturers to achieve economies of scale without having sizable overseas sales because, as the chairman said in his opening remarks, 95 percent of the world lives outside the United States. So when financing for foreign trade is impaired, the whole enterprise suffers.

Sixth, we will lose the most important ally of U.S. commercial banks and other private lenders in assuming the risk of financing foreign trade. Almost all of Ex-Im's transactions, 98 percent, involve commercial financial institutions, and, in many cases, those institutions could not participate without Ex-Im loans, guarantees, or insurance.

Seventh, we will lose the level playing field that Ex-Im provides for U.S. exporters when it steps in to counter the predatory financing of state-supported foreign competitors. China has become especially active in assisting its exporters to undercut U.S. sales in third markets by extending financing on concessionary terms, and Ex-Im works constantly to counter such unfair practices.

Eight, we will lose the main point of leverage that America has in deterring other countries from pursuing unfair practices in their own export financing. Because foreign companies and credit agencies know that Ex-Im might step in to counter predatory practices, they are less likely to engage in market-distorting activity.

I might mention that the Financial Times, Britain's most respected newspaper, opined last year that it would be odd were the United States to disarm unilaterally by abandoning one of the few tools it possesses for disciplining the behavior of trading partners.

Ninth, we will lose one of the very few agencies in Washington that is a bargain, an agency that doesn't cost taxpayers a cent and, in fact, sends hundreds of millions of dollars to the Treasury every year while sustaining thousands of jobs in the export sector.

And, finally, if Ex-Im goes down, there is one other thing that we will lose: A political discourse based on rational analysis rather than unbending ideology. The arguments for killing Ex-Im are illogical and they are fact-free, whereas the case for keeping it is empirically and analytically overwhelming.

There is nothing wrong with espousing the principle of limited government, but in the case of the Export-Import Bank, we should listen to Winston Churchill, arguably the most important Western leader of the 20th century, who observed, "The duty of government is to be, first of all, practical." I would not sacrifice my own generation to a principle.

Thank you.

[The prepared statement of Mr. Thompson follows:]

LOSING EX-IM BANK WOULD BE BAD FOR EVERYBODY

Statement before the Subcommittee on Terrorism, Non-Proliferation and Trade of the House Foreign Affairs Committee

Loren B. Thompson
Lexington Institute
October 23, 2015

I have been asked to assess the consequences of failing to reauthorize the Export-Import Bank, which has been a significant contributor to U.S. trade competitiveness for 80 years.

The bank's authority to extend new credit only lapsed four months ago, so it's a bit early to be describing the fallout.

My statement will therefore focus on consequences that can be confidently predicted in the years ahead if no reauthorization occurs and the bank has to unwind its programs.

Near as I can tell, there will be no gains to the nation if Ex-Im goes away...

-- Taxpayers won't save any money, because Ex-Im already pays for itself.

-- The government won't get smaller, because other steps will need to be taken to level the playing field for U.S. exports.

-- And the economy won't become more competitive, because it will operate at a disadvantage with countries still providing export credit.

So the consequences of shutting down the Export-Import Bank are negative for pretty much everybody -- except maybe our trade rivals.

I will therefore devote the balance of my remarks to what America will lose if Ex-Im permanently ceases operations.

First, we will lose America's sole export credit agency.

Every major trading nation has a government agency dedicated to mitigating risk and facilitating financing of foreign trade.

America would be the only big industrial country without such an agency, leaving its exporters dependent on private lenders who have already stated they will not fill the vacuum created by Ex-Im's demise.

Second, we will lose global market share in key industries.

Many overseas buyers require government guarantees as a condition of bidding, which U.S. exporters could no longer secure.

Even if such guarantees were not required, foreign customers would find it easier to obtain financing on favorable terms from countries with export credit agencies, so that is where they would go for their jetliners, earth movers and locomotives.

Third, we will lose more ground in the U.S. trade balance at a time when America's non-petroleum trade deficit is already the worst on record.

The tidal wave of foreign goods reaching these shores has reduced our growth rate by a full percentage point in recent quarters, and allowing Ex-Im to die would make that problem worse.

Fourth, we will lose tens of thousands of jobs as companies like Boeing and GE see overseas sales decline, and hundreds of smaller companies are forced to abandon exporting entirely.

Initially, the job losses would come within the companies and among their suppliers, but additional job losses would occur indirectly as money once spent by export workers was no longer available to pay grocers, teachers, and other providers in their communities.

Fifth, we will lose even more of America's domestic manufacturing base, which once was said to be the arsenal of democracy but now has shrunk to a mere 12% of the economy.

It isn't feasible anymore for big manufacturers to achieve economies of scale without having sizable overseas sales, so when financing for foreign trade is impaired, the whole enterprise suffers.

Sixth, we will lose the most important ally of U.S. commercial banks and other private lenders in assuming the risk of financing foreign trade.

Almost all of Ex-Im's transactions -- about 98% -- involve commercial financial institutions that in many cases could not participate without Ex-Im loans, guarantees or insurance.

Seventh, we will lose the level playing field that Ex-Im provides for U.S. exporters when it steps in to counter the predatory financing of state-supported foreign competitors.

China has become especially active in assisting its exporters to undercut U.S. sales in third markets by extending financing on concessionary terms, and Ex-Im works constantly to counter such unfair practices.

Eighth, we will lose the main point of leverage that America has in deterring other countries from pursuing unfair practices in their own export financing.

Because foreign companies and credit agencies know that Ex-Im might step in to counter predatory trading practices, they are less likely to engage in market-distorting activity.

The Financial Times, Britain's most respected newspaper, opined last year that "it would be odd were the U.S. to disarm unilaterally" by abandoning one of the few tools it possesses for disciplining the behavior of trading partners.

Ninth, we will lose one of the very few agencies in Washington that is a bargain -- an agency that doesn't cost taxpayers a cent and in fact sends hundreds of millions of dollars to the Treasury every year, while sustaining thousands of jobs in the export sector.

Washington is full of agencies that waste money on dubious missions and outdated practices, but the Export-Import Bank isn't one of them.

Finally, if Ex-Im goes down, there is one other thing that we will lose -- a political discourse based on rational analysis rather than mindless ideology.

The arguments for killing Ex-Im are illogical and fact-free, whereas the case for keeping it is empirically and analytically overwhelming.

There's nothing wrong with espousing the principle of limited government, but in the case of the Export-Import Bank, we should listen to Winston Churchill, arguably the greatest Western leader of the last century, who observed...

The duty of governments is to be first of all practical... I would not sacrifice my own generation to a principle.

Mr. POE. I thank all of our witnesses.

I will recognize myself for 5 minutes of questions.

Mr. Schroeder, may I ask you about your small business? And, yes, I know where Olney, Texas, is, and only because I was lost going to Abilene and I found it.

You heard Ms. Katz say that Ex-Im Bank, the taxpayers are on the hook, it is a subsidy to businesses. Would you comment on that, if you can, from your point of view as a small business?

Mr. SCHROEDER. Absolutely.

Well, the argument that it is a subsidy has never really made much sense to us at Air Tractor in Olney. We pay very good money for this particular product. It is the only thing that we have to be able to compete in our emerging markets. And a lot of people don't understand the——

Mr. POE. Explain it. Explain it then. Make it simple. I know you are a financial guy, but make it simple.

Mr. SCHROEDER. So the argument against the subsidy, basically, is Air Tractor has paid over 1 million U.S. dollars each year for the past several years. As a matter of fact, in the past 4, we have paid 4.8 million U.S. dollars to the U.S. Government for this Medium-Term Credit Insurance Program, and we have never lost a dime on it.

Mr. POE. Do you pay a fee to use Ex-Im Bank?

Mr. SCHROEDER. We pay a fee on every single—every single aircraft that we sell with Ex-Im support is attached to an insurance policy, and we pay a premium on every single insurance policy.

Mr. POE. Do you partner with a private bank?

Mr. SCHROEDER. Absolutely, on the back end.

Mr. POE. Like Amegy sitting next to you. So you not only pay a fee to Ex-Im to use that service, you also partner with a U.S. bank, a local bank, community bank normally, to—for what purpose? Why do you partner with a bank like Amegy?

Mr. SCHROEDER. Well, because we are not a bank. We don't have the ability—we extend the financing, but we can't hold it on our balance sheet. We don't have the capacity to do that. So we turn around and sell that bank to a U.S. commercial bank, who then collects from our customer with interest. So, yes, we are getting business through Ex-Im Bank; we are giving business to the U.S. banks as well.

Mr. POE. And who is paying the interest?

Mr. SCHROEDER. The customer is.

Mr. POE. In Brazil, primarily.

Mr. SCHROEDER. Yes, in our South American emerging markets, the customers.

Mr. POE. Okay.

You use Ex-Im Bank to sell those crop dusters. And I assume you didn't fly one of those up here to Washington.

Mr. SCHROEDER. No.

Mr. POE. Have you had any job loss because you don't have Ex-Im?

Mr. SCHROEDER. That is tough to say. So, naturally, businesses are going to be kind of resolute in laying people off. You know, that is a last-ditch effort for us. We are going to try to maintain our employment base as is for as long as possible.

Mr. POE. Have you lost sales?

Mr. SCHROEDER. Yes, absolutely, we have lost sales.

Mr. POE. You were selling 16 of those planes to Brazil, and you were able to sell 6 now. Is that what you said?

Mr. SCHROEDER. Yes, sir. And last year we sold 28 aircraft, I believe, into the Brazilian market. This year we will probably do eight or nine.

Mr. POE. And, as far as jobs, if the current trend occurs in your business, you think maybe there might be a possibility of people losing their job at Air Tractor?

Mr. SCHROEDER. Absolutely. We have been able to sustain them this year because we have put a short-term patch together and taken a lot of risk on the company. But if next year's export season comes around, we have no idea. There will be——

Mr. POE. What do people do? Do they build these airplanes? Is that what they do?

Mr. SCHROEDER. Yes, we build everything by hand. So it is 100 percent made in Olney, Texas.

Mr. POE. And what do these planes do? What are they are? Are they for crop dusting?

Mr. SCHROEDER. They are for crop dusting. Agricultural airplanes is our bread and butter, obviously. So big yellow and blue airplanes that you see flying around spraying crops.

Mr. POE. All right.

Ms. Katz, let me ask you a couple of questions. You did use the terms ''a subsidy,'' the taxpayer is on the hook, so to speak, and ''government-based.''

I assume that you have a bank account somewhere?

Ms. KATZ. Yes.

Mr. POE. I am not going to ask you where. We are not going to advertise for them.

Now, whatever you have put in that bank as an individual, the Federal Government guarantees that deposit up to $250,000. That is right?

Ms. KATZ. Yes.

Mr. POE. So isn't that a government-backed program of financing but for an individual at an American bank? Isn't that a government-backed program, the FDIC?

Ms. KATZ. It is, and it is one that I would argue could be better managed through the private sector.

Mr. POE. And you don't have a problem——

Ms. KATZ. If I could explain what the subsidy is——

Mr. POE. Excuse me. I am reclaiming my time because we only have a few minutes.

It is an insurance program that if the bank goes insolvent, that the customer, the depositor, the Federal Government will back that deposit up to $250,000. It is a government-backed program for an individual. I don't know that Americans have any problem accepting that insurance program.

And, Mr. Raguso, last question. Isn't that what Ex-Im Bank does too? It insures a loan on a project but goes through a private bank as well?

Mr. RAGUSO. It does. It does.You know, premiums are paid, or guarantee fees are paid. And this is, kind of, the risk-sharing that happens between a private bank and the Ex-Im Bank.

Mr. POE. All right. My time has expired.

I yield to the gentleman from Massachusetts, Mr. Keating.

Mr. KEATING. Thank you, Mr. Chairman.

I think, Mr. Schroeder, if we were flying one of your planes over our district, one of the things you would see is these huge crops of red that are cranberries. And when you are talking about big con- glomerates, I just wanted to share briefly the experience of the cranberry industry, whether it is Massachusetts or Wisconsin.

They have been successful in terms of supply, and, because of that, they have either had to shrink, lose profits, or diminish their own markets. But they have had the opportunity to find markets where they never existed before, in Asia and in Europe, places where there is no word for ''cranberry'' and where getting conven- tional financing is nearly impossible for something there is no word for. Yet we have continued to grow in our country on this because of the Ex-Im Bank, because we gave that opportunity initially.

So I just wanted to clarify, these are small businesses, and whether it is what Mr. Heck, you know, said in terms of Boeing, Mr. Thompson said in terms of Boeing, those are small, medium American businesses that are affected.

Now, there is one thing that Mr. Thompson mentioned that I think is very important to maybe elaborate on, and that is the fact that the role of the Ex-Im Bank is—one of the things that just doesn't jump out at you is, in the marketplace, they are there to provide an alternative, a credible alternative, one that doesn't en- gage in practices that are engaged in in other countries, sort of a referee or an alternative or at least an option that brings the rest of the market competitively to where it should be.

And you mentioned some of the predatory practices that are there. In the absence of Ex-Im, what kind of actions do you think— and ''unfair advantage'' is a better word, maybe—that some of these foreign export credit agencies, what will they have over American businesses? And what are the kind of things you see or you would see more of in terms of these predatory practices if there wasn't an Ex-Im alternative?

Mr. THOMPSON. Congressman, because we are now a relatively small part of the global economy, barely 20 percent of economic output around the world, we have to sell overseas in order to achieve the economies of scale necessary to be on pricing parity with foreign competitors.

But what will happen is, if there is not access to Ex-Im loan fa- cilities, guarantees, and so on in countries that are considered high- risk, like Pakistan, like Ethiopia, like nearly 100 other coun- tries you could mention, then they will just naturally turn to the Europeans, they will turn to China. And so locomotive sales from Erie, Pennsylvania, will dry up to a point where they will no longer be competitive.

China has recently, with its own export-import bank, proposed to lead the construction of high-speed rail in California—in Cali- fornia—because they are willing to front the money to do that. Small companies, even medium- and large-size companies, can't compete with a foreign government. They have to have the assistance of the U.S. Government, particularly in those markets where it is not feasible for the local economic system, the financial structures, to support a large-size loan or it is just outside the risk profile of the private sector.

In that regard, I would just like to mention, this is not a subsidy. The World Trade Organization requires that export credit agencies be self-sustaining so they will not be subsidies.

Mr. KEATING. Well, thank you.

And Ms. Katz mentioned that 98 percent of the reason that business transactions occur aren't dealing with the Export-Import Bank. And I will take our country and place it competitively against these countries any day on the 98 percent, but because of this one leverage point, we are not getting on the playing field to compete.

Mr. THOMPSON. Right.

Mr. KEATING. We are not allowed to compete on the 98 percent——

Mr. THOMPSON. Right.

Mr. KEATING [continuing]. Of the reasons people choose from another country to buy American products. And that is the critical point.

And I think Mr. Raguso mentioned this a little bit too, or Mr. Thompson. This program also helps support traditional private American financing, because there is available financing, but a lot of that wouldn't exist if the Ex-Im Bank wasn't there for that one——

Mr. THOMPSON. That is exactly right.

Mr. KEATING [continuing]. That one space that is necessary in the transaction.

Mr. THOMPSON. A typical Ex-Im transaction is brought to the Bank by a private lender. They just need the support of the Ex-Im Bank in order to achieve an acceptable risk profile.

Like, for example, if there is a danger somebody in Pakistan will default, Ex-Im will guarantee, for a fee, that that default would be covered. It is not a high risk; they make a big profit every year. But because they are willing to make that guarantee, the private lender can extend the credit, knowing that it is not outside of what they are allowed to——

Mr. KEATING. This helps the private financing stay in the U.S.——

Mr. THOMPSON. Exactly.

Mr. KEATING [continuing]. Banks, not in foreign banks.

I yield back.

Mr. POE. I thank the gentleman.

Without objection, the Chair will introduce into the record statements by 80 business owners throughout the United States on how Ex-Im Bank affects them and/or the failure to reauthorize has hurt their businesses.

The Chair will now recognize the gentleman from Pennsylvania, Mr. Perry.

Mr. PERRY. Thank you, Mr. Chairman.

Mr. Raguso, what risk does the bank accept in partnering with Ex-Im and a business like Mr. Schroeder's?

Mr. RAGUSO. Right, so I will speak primarily from the perspective of our bank and the programs that we use.

In a working capital loan, we access this working capital guarantee program that Ex-Im has. It provides a 90-percent guarantee on the loan that we make to our customer. And so, in that circumstance, you know, we are——

Mr. PERRY. You are accepting a 10-percent share of the risk? Is that what you are saying?

Mr. RAGUSO. Right. Right.

Mr. PERRY. All right.

Mr. RAGUSO. But the bigger picture is that Ex-Im, as a solution, is not something that we offer in isolation. It is part of a relationship, a lot of credit that we offer our customers. So, typically, on our portfolio of Ex-Im business, the loans that we make that are Ex-Im-backed represent about half of what we lend to a customer. So we have a broader relationship.

So it is not as if we make an Ex-Im loan and something happens to that loan and we move on down the road. If a loan goes past due, it affects all of the lending that we do to a customer.

Mr. PERRY. I understand that, but the risk is what the risk is. It is what it is, right? It is 10 percent in that scenario that you just gave.

Mr. RAGUSO. On that particular thing, yes.

Mr. PERRY. Okay.

All right. Ms. Katz, what percentage of Ex-Im financing did you say goes to the top 10? What was that statistic? Fifty-one percent or something like that?

Ms. KATZ. That was 51 percent between the years 2007 and 2014.

Mr. PERRY. Okay. To who?

Ms. KATZ. I could read you the list of the top——

Mr. PERRY. No, no. Just what was—so the top 10 Fortune—what was——

Ms. KATZ. Fifty-one percent went to just 10 companies.

Mr. PERRY. Just 10 companies.

Ms. KATZ. Right.

Mr. PERRY. Okay.

What appropriate reforms have been requested of the Ex-Im Bank regarding small-business loans but have not been implemented, if you know?

In other words, one of the problems or one of the—I will maybe call it a problem, a challenge, or a criticism of Ex-Im is that it claims all this small-business activity, but when you have 51 percent going to only 10 companies—and I imagine they are probably large companies. I don't want to take that for granted, but I am just supposing they are.

What reforms have been requested either in past legislation that has been signed but not enacted or in current legislation that you know of?

Ms. KATZ. Most of the reforms that I am referring to in my testimony have to do with the operations of Ex-Im in terms of managing risk, in terms of transparency, in terms of how their operations are monitored.

I have an entire study about this. I would be glad to forward that to——

Mr. PERRY. Sure. But——

Ms. KATZ [continuing]. You. But the GAO and the inspector general have issued a number of reports over the years pointing out systemic flaws within Ex-Im in terms of its operations as well as in its, you know, risk management.

Mr. PERRY. Right. And I agree with you, and I accept that. But I guess my point is, of all the serious reforms that have been proffered, none are really dealing with making sure that Ex-Im supports small businesses like Mr. Schroeder's here more than what they currently do. It is all process, which is fine, but nothing really to require them to do more in the small-business market that you know of.

Ms. KATZ. That I know of. But the problem is that what Ex-Im calls a small business and what the rest of the world calls a——

Mr. PERRY. Right.

Ms. KATZ [continuing]. Small business is very different.

Mr. PERRY. And I was thinking that, as well. I just want to keep moving here.

Let me ask you this. There has been a number of indictments at the Ex-Im Bank. Do private banks have the same level of indictments and board-member involvement, board-member-on-the-Bank involvement with the same companies that the Bank is lending to? Do regular commercial banks or private banks or financial institutions have the same level of criminal or alleged criminal activity or nepotism between the financial institution and the receiving institutions?

Ms. KATZ. I don't know, but what I can say is that, if you are managing public funds, funds that aren't your own, that I would hope you would have the highest level of security and risk management rather than just what is average.

Mr. PERRY. Well, I mean, do you know what the percentage is of board members on the Bank that also have involvement with the people that they are lending to, the companies or the concerns?

Ms. KATZ. No, I don't.

Mr. PERRY. I think there was testimony in a recent hearing in this committee that it is upward of 50 percent, just to remind everybody what we heard here.

And I think, what, 13 current pending indictments or something like that? Are you familiar with that?

Ms. KATZ. The last I checked, I think that there were 47 active investigations.

Mr. PERRY. Okay.

All right. My time has expired. I yield.

Mr. POE. The gentleman's time has expired. Thank you.

Ms. Katz, you referred to a document, a report, analysis that you wrote. Would you make that available to the committee?

Ms. KATZ. Absolutely.

Mr. POE. I am not talking about the GAO report. We will get that.

Ms. KATZ. No, no.

Mr. POE. Based on what Mr. Perry said, and make that a part of the record, without objection.

Ms. KATZ. Absolutely.

Mr. POE. All right. The Chair recognizes the gentleman from California, Mr. Sherman.

Mr. SHERMAN. I would point out there are more allegations about government agencies than the private sector because the press covers government agencies, we have political disputes about government agencies, we have theological and ideological disputes about the existence of government agencies. So I would expect that there would be a lot more articles, scrutiny, and allegations.

We should point out that when a big company, a big American company exports, it usually has supported hundreds of small businesses buying the parts. And even if you care not at all about Airbus or Boeing and only care about small companies, there are a lot more small companies, American small companies, selling to Boeing than selling to Airbus.

This isn't a practical dispute. This is a theological dispute. The holy scriptures of libertarianism have no place in their sacred novels for an entity like Export-Import Bank because they create a perfect world, an ideologically pure world. I would like to live in such a world—maybe not their world, but a world just as pure.

Ms. Katz, what is your organization doing to cause Europe and Asia and China to drop their finance authorities? Or do you really imagine a world in which every one of our competitors has subsidized financing and we don't?

Ms. KATZ. Well, first, I will say that I don't base my policy recommendations on what I imagine but on what the empirical evidence shows me.

That said, it has been the United States policy with respect to Ex-Im to negotiate with OECD countries to eliminate the use of export credit agencies——

Mr. SHERMAN. If I can interrupt, where would I get any leverage to do that?

Look, I gave over 100 speeches for George McGovern. If anybody here can be accused of advocating unilateral military disarmament, it might be me. I was a teenager, and I didn't go that far. And I hung out with some people who really believed that if we didn't have a military other countries wouldn't.

How would we possibly persuade other countries to cut back if we had nothing to trade in return?

Ms. KATZ. We have a lot to trade in return. And the idea that there is unilateral disarmament here is just wrong. I am——

Mr. SHERMAN. So what would you offer the Japanese to get rid of their subsidized financing for their exports if we already didn't have an Export-Import Bank? Should we——

Ms. KATZ. I am not going to try to make——

Mr. SHERMAN. Should we write them a check every year from the taxpayers?

Ms. KATZ. I am not going to try to make the Chinese do anything. What I am going to say is that the United States is better off than Japan is if we don't offer subsidies. Because, you know, subsidies, on the whole, detract from the overall economic benefit of countries. So if——

Mr. SHERMAN. Okay. So you are trying to sell a U.S. product, and you have a strong European or Asian competitor. The products might be equal, the price might be equal. One side has concessionary financing; the other doesn't. Why in the world would somebody fail to buy the foreign product if it was just as good and it came with better financing?

Ms. KATZ. Well, if it is just as good is open to great question, but as I said before——

Mr. SHERMAN. Okay, look, I love American companies. Yes, all of our products are better. But the fact is that there are circumstances where we face tough competition and our product is just as good as the competitor, not better.

Ms. KATZ. This is sort of illogical, because if you are going to say that, then we should be financing every single product that we sell overseas.

Mr. SHERMAN. Only when we face concessionary financing and competition.

Ms. KATZ. We should do it with everything. In China, we cannot keep up with China's subsidies, and so——

Mr. SHERMAN. We are talking here about export financing——

Ms. KATZ. I know.

Mr. SHERMAN [continuing]. Where we face not only from one country like China, we face from every major competitor.

And the idea that products don't sell because of the financing package, just watch a sports game. How many commercials are you going to see advertising this car or that car, U.S. and foreign, where the focus of the commercial is not on torque, it is not even on cup holders, it is on the leasing terms, it is on the financing terms. And I would say that it may very well be that a Ford and a Chevy are equal, but one comes with better financing.

Ms. KATZ. You are presuming that the decision on a product is made based on its financing. And as I indicated earlier——

Mr. SHERMAN. Everybody who is watching a sports game comes to that conclusion when it comes to buying what they buy with financing, and that is an automobile.

Ms. KATZ. I am not sure that is exactly true.

Mr. POE. The gentleman's time has expired.

The Chair recognizes another gentleman from California, Mr. Rohrabacher.

Mr. ROHRABACHER. Unilateral disarmament. My gosh, Brad, that is a fantastic admission.

Mr. SHERMAN. It is an admission that I knew some people.

Mr. ROHRABACHER. All right.

I would like to ask, I guess—is it ''Raguso''? Is that how you pronounce this?

Mr. RAGUSO. Yes.

Mr. ROHRABACHER. Thank you. Mr. Raguso, we just came to the fact that the bankers, of which you are representing the financial interests, take only 10 percent of the risk of these loans that are going to selected people who get this subsidy. What percentage of the profit of that loan does the private bank get?

Mr. RAGUSO. Right. So I guess to clarify, I am speaking about one Ex-Im program—there are many—but the program that is used by my bank, which is designed to help small U.S. exporters export their product competitively and unlock collateral that would otherwise be unavailable.

Mr. ROHRABACHER. Okay. So that doesn't include the big guys, then.

Mr. RAGUSO. What is that?

Mr. ROHRABACHER. You are saying it is just the small guys.

Mr. RAGUSO. Well, the way——

Mr. ROHRABACHER. Because the big guys are—51 percent of the loans, at least, we know, go to the 10 major corporations, so I assume they are the big guys. But you are only talking about little guys, then.

Mr. RAGUSO. I am talking about, again, the programs that we access, where, again, our customer is the U.S. exporter.

Mr. ROHRABACHER. Okay. And what percentage of the profit do you get of those loans?

Mr. RAGUSO. Right. So, after we charge an Ex-Im Bank fee, which ranges in today's world anywhere from 1.25 percent to 1.75 percent——

Mr. ROHRABACHER. Right.

Mr. RAGUSO. You know, our bank makes the loan. And so those fees go to Ex-Im, we make the loan, and so the interest income on the loan——

Mr. ROHRABACHER. But 90 percent of the loan, of course, is being guaranteed, you have no risk whatsoever, but you assume 10 percent of the risk. How much of the profit from that loan goes to your bank?

Mr. RAGUSO. A hundred percent of the profit.

Mr. ROHRABACHER. Oh, all right. So we get 100 percent of the profit but 10 percent of the risk. Ah, I think there are a lot of businesses that would love to have that kind of relationship with the government.

Why is it that certain businesses have that right but other businesses don't?

Mr. RAGUSO. Right. So——

Mr. ROHRABACHER. Is it just size? Are we talking about every big business in America has that right to have that type of guarantee, a subsidy, as Ms. Katz is saying? Oh, no, somebody has to select them. I wonder if they select people that are close to them. Oh, wait a minute, there is an investigation going on to that.

You say 47 people are being investigated now, Ms. Katz, for some sort of conflict of interest there on choosing who gets those loans? Is that right?

Ms. KATZ. The nature of each of those investigations varies.

Mr. ROHRABACHER. Right. All right.

Well, let me note, what we have here is—I am sorry, you can call it ''principle'' if you want, but I think it is also practical that when we decide to set up a system in which certain people like this gentleman will get all the profit but only assume 10 percent of the risk, I think that is an insult to the rest of the American people who are trying to be enterprisers and have to assume all the risk for the things they do in order to make a profit.

And Ms. Katz's arguments, I don't consider that to be philosophical. I consider that to be also something that is very practical in terms of the people who don't get the money——

Mr. THOMPSON. Well, Congressman, you understand that anybody——

Mr. ROHRABACHER [continuing]. Who don't get the subsidy.

Please go right ahead.

Mr. THOMPSON [continuing]. Can apply for these financial benefits if they comply with the standards established by Congress in the charter. Anybody can. It is not——

Mr. ROHRABACHER. No, anybody can't. You are——

Mr. THOMPSON [continuing]. Hoarding of benefits.

Mr. ROHRABACHER. First of all, anybody can't get it. They have to be selected and go through the process. And, as we have heard, it is possible that the people involved in the process might take their self-interest into consideration, which happens, by the way, every time you get a big government program.

One last note here, Mr. Chairman, and that is: How is this different than the actual guarantee that we put on people's bank accounts? All right. You know, Ms. Katz has a certain amount of money in her savings, and that is guaranteed. The difference is every American is eligible for that——every single American.

What we have here is crony capitalism. And I am happy that you have a company that is all employee-owned. I am a big supporter of employee ownership. I want to encourage that. But there are other companies down the road that might want to get that subsidy as well. And the fact is that we are picking and choosing who is going to be the winner and who——and especially the banks are the big winners in all of this.

Thank you very much, Mr. Chairman.

Mr. POE. Thank you, Mr. Rohrabacher.

The Chair now recognizes Mr. Heck from Washington.

Mr. HECK. Thank you, Mr. Chairman. Thank you very much for the privilege to be here today.

First, fact check time. In fact, the Kirk-Heitkamp bill and that which we will vote on Monday night does change the small-business formula and increases the minimum requirement from 20 percent to 25 percent.

Fact check two: The previous legislation does not require negotiating the elimination of ECAs. It requires the negotiation of eliminating subsidies. And there are no subsidies. Well, that is not true. That is not true. The Ex-Im subsidizes the Federal Government for a generation in billions of dollars transferred.

Fact three: Not a single member of the board of directors of the Ex-Im works for or is on the board of directors of a company that receives financing——not a single member.

Look, I have heard a lot of arguments over a long period of time, and here is the harsh and blunt conclusion I have come to: To accept the arguments of the opponent is the equivalent, the moral equivalent, of looking Mr. Raguso and Mr. Schroeder in the eye and saying to them, "You are either stupid or lying." And I absolutely know that that is not the truth today.

In fact, Mr. Schroeder, there is no person on the face of the earth in the last 3 years who has listened to more witnesses on this issue. You have done the finest job of reflecting and representing your company of anybody I have ever heard. I commend you for your eloquence and for your heartfelt testimony.

More importantly, you go home to Olney, Texas, and, as a proud son of Texas, I want you to tell the 270 employees that an overwhelming majority of the Members of the House of Representatives are not going to stop until we reauthorize the Export-Import Bank, including the chair of this subcommittee and the ranking member. Help is on the way, Mr. Schroeder.

Dr. Thompson, first of all, it is 85-percent minimum domestic content, sir, if I may correct you.

Mr. THOMPSON. Correct.

Mr. HECK. Secondly, the purpose of today's hearing is to discuss the impact on the economy of the disappearance of the Ex-Im. But insofar as this is the Foreign Affairs Committee, I would like to actually take the conversation in a slightly different direction, and that is the issue of our Nation's security and its defense.

Let me lay out just a couple or three beliefs on my part—some are facts, some are beliefs—and have you respond to the question.

Boeing and GE constitute the heart of this Nation's manufacturing base. And, by the way, I don't know how often I have to say: Supply chain, supply chain, supply chain. An appalling lack of understanding of the private economy, that there are 8,000 small businesses behind the Boeing Company.

Number two, China is now the second-largest economy in the world and a fierce competitor of ours.

Number three, China is aggressively involved in expansion of its interest to the building of islands and in the market. Code named C919, they are building a wide-body aircraft to compete with Airbus and the Boeing Company.

All that said, Dr. Thompson, impact on economy aside, is there an impact on our Nation's security and defense if we indeed unilaterally disarm in the export credit authority world? And if so, how would you describe it?

Mr. THOMPSON. Well, it is a complicated question, but to just offer a simple answer, Ex-Im's benefits accrue primarily to companies that are in the business of exporting capital equipment, like jetliners, like locomotives—the big, expensive things that are hard for foreign buyers and countries to afford. It is in precisely those sorts of technologies where we put much of our defense acquisition dollars.

Mr. HECK. From some of these same companies.

Mr. THOMPSON. Right. Exactly. In fact, there is definitely a multiplier effect and an economy of scale at places like Boeing. Because a lot of future aircraft for the Pentagon will be leveraged off of commercial transports. So if Boeing becomes less efficient, if it loses economies of scale, then it will cost the Pentagon more.

At some point, though, you get forced out of markets entirely. I saw this happen in my hometown of Plymouth, where, one after another, the factories closed because of foreign competition. Not unnecessarily unfair competition, but, you know, we live in a country where people don't make penicillin or flatware or rebar anymore. Eventually, you get forced out of markets entirely, and then your defense establishment becomes dependent on potential enemies for things it must have to win a war.

Mr. HECK. Exactly. Thank you, sir.

Mr. ROHRABACHER. Would the gentleman yield for a question before your time is up?

Mr. HECK. With the chair's indulgence, as I am out of time.

Mr. POE. A short question, Mr. Rohrabacher.

Mr. ROHRABACHER. You would concede that those of us asking tough questions do not assume that those people who disagree with us or have answers that we consider to be wrong—you would concede that we can respect people who we disagree with and don't consider them stupid or lying.

Mr. HECK. I certainly respect you, sir, even though we disagree on a lot.

Mr. ROHRABACHER. Right, but you would agree——

Mr. POE. The gentleman's time has expired.

Mr. ROHRABACHER [continuing]. But you would agree that is not——

Mr. POE. The gentleman's time has expired.

Mr. ROHRABACHER. Thank you very much.

Mr. POE. The Chair recognizes the gentlelady from Wisconsin for 5 minutes.

Ms. MOORE. Thank you so much, Chairman Poe, for this extraordinary opportunity to sit on this panel.

I want to thank the witnesses for appearing today for this very important discussion of our economy.

My name is Gwen Moore, and I hail from Milwaukee, Wisconsin. And I am old enough to remember the glory days of Milwaukee being sort of the manufacturing center of the universe, where our economy was based on producing the most tanned leather, steel, iron ore—the glory days of the great, huge factories like A.O. Smith and Allis-Chalmers. And so now Milwaukee still relies on manufacturing, but it is struggling.

So I can understand, to some extent, the argument that has often been made about the Ex-Im Bank only supporting, sort of, large corporations like GE or Boeing. And, of course, we are losing 350 jobs out of GE because of the lack of financing from Ex-Im Bank. But what I want to make sure that the panel understands is that Milwaukee and many other places in the United States are no longer in those glory days.

And so I would ask, first of all, Ms. Katz—and excuse me if I have missed some of your testimony. I have a company in my district called Maxon, and, you know, they make mining equipment. They are part of the supply chain you have heard about, and they say they absolutely cannot function without Ex-Im Bank. They have 30 employees. Part of their supply chain is a group right down the street that has four employees.

And we heard testimony here—I think my colleague Mr. Heck just mentioned that Boeing alone has 8,000 companies in their supply chain.

And so I guess I am wondering—I am confused—are you advocating that if the Maxons of the world can't make it that we ought to just let them wither on the vine? Is that your testimony today?

Ms. KATZ. What I am saying and pointing out is that without Ex-Im it is wrong to presume that there won't be other avenues of financing that would keep these supply chains going. And, in fact, for the biggest beneficiaries of Ex-Im, they have years and years of back orders to keep these suppliers, you know, working.

Now, in terms of anecdotes, like you are bringing up in your district, you know, anecdotes are heart-tugging, there is no question about it, but the small business that you refer to is only half the equation. The other half of the equation is the company that is not getting the subsidy.

And, Congressman Heck, I will explain to you what the subsidy is, because there is an——

Ms. MOORE. Okay, well, this is my time. It is not Mr. Heck's time. Thank you so much for that.

So you are saying there is some other way, and you don't necessarily know what that other way is.

Ms. KATZ. No, I do. I know exactly what the other way is. It is the way that 98 percent of other exporters do it, which is through private financing.

Ms. MOORE. With their own money or something.

Ms. KATZ. Well, they borrow. Some use their own money. There are various bonding——

Ms. MOORE. Okay.

So who on the panel is for the TPP? I guess I want to know how the TPP might be impacted by the lack of an export credit agency. Who supports the TPP?

No one?

Ms. KATZ. I don't speak on that.

Ms. MOORE. Okay.

Mr. Raguso?

Mr. RAGUSO. I am not an expert on TPP. All I would say is, you know, for our customers, more trade means more business for their businesses. And so you could say I am not trying to, I guess, join the two together, but, yet again, freer trade means more opportunities for our customers.

Ms. MOORE. Okay.

And just in my last 20 seconds, who can answer the question— I was talking to Ms. Katz. The 2 percent of the businesses that need this financing, what kinds of businesses are they?

Ms. KATZ. The data is in my testimony, but about 80 percent of the Ex-Im financing is benefiting larger companies.

Ms. MOORE. This is a dollar amount. It is not because they are big.

Ms. KATZ. Well, but what we care about is the money.

Ms. MOORE. No, we care about the—well, I care about the two employees in my district that get decent wages every day.

Mr. THOMPSON. Could I clarify something?

Ms. KATZ. Can we fix every problem that every person in America has? I don't think so.

Mr. THOMPSON. Ninety percent of the transactions that Ex-Im did last year were small-business transactions.

Ms. MOORE. Right.

Mr. THOMPSON. Nearly 40 percent, by volume, of the exports were small-business exports. Roughly 25 percent of the actual money that was disbursed or the benefits that were disbursed went to small business. And that is not counting all the small businesses that support companies like Boeing or General Electric.

Ms. MOORE. Thank you so much.

My time has expired. I want to thank the chairman for his indulgence.

Mr. POE. I thank the members of the committee and the guests of the committee that came to inquire about this issue. I think the testimony of all four witnesses was excellent. Appreciate your expertise in this area.

And this subcommittee is adjourned. Thank you again.

[Whereupon, at 10:52 a.m., the subcommittee was adjourned.]

A P P E N D I X

Material Submitted for the Record

SUBCOMMITTEE HEARING NOTICE
COMMITTEE ON FOREIGN AFFAIRS
U.S. HOUSE OF REPRESENTATIVES
WASHINGTON, DC 20515-6128

Subcommittee on Terrorism, Nonproliferation, and Trade
Ted Poe (R-TX), Chairman

TO: MEMBERS OF THE COMMITTEE ON FOREIGN AFFAIRS

You are respectfully requested to attend an OPEN hearing of the Committee on Foreign Affairs, to be held by the Subcommittee on Terrorism, Nonproliferation, and Trade in Room 2172 of the Rayburn House Office Building (and available live on the Committee website at http://www.ForeignAffairs.house.gov):

DATE: Friday, October 23, 2015

TIME: 9:30 a.m.

SUBJECT: Evaluating the Export-Import Bank in the Global Economy

WITNESSES: Ms. Diane Katz
                   Senior Research Fellow in Regulatory Policy
                   The Institute for Economic Freedom and Opportunity
                   The Heritage Foundation

                   Mr. T.J. Raguso
                   Executive Vice President
                   International Division
                   Amegy Bank National Association

                   Mr. Tyler Schroeder
                   Financial Analyst
                   Air Tractor Inc.

                   Mr. Loren B. Thompson, Ph.D.
                   Chief Operating Officer
                   Lexington Institute

By Direction of the Chairman

The Committee on Foreign Affairs seeks to make its facilities accessible to persons with disabilities. If you are in need of special accommodations, please call 202/225-5021 at least four business days in advance of the event, whenever practicable. Questions with regard to special accommodations in general (including availability of Committee materials in alternative formats and assistive listening devices) may be directed to the Committee.

COMMITTEE ON FOREIGN AFFAIRS

MINUTES OF SUBCOMMITTEE ON _____ *Terrorism Nonproliferation and Trade* _____ HEARING

Day ___*Friday*___ Date ___*October 23*___ Room ___*2172*___

Starting Time ___*9:38 a.m.*___ Ending Time ___*10:52 a.m.*___

Recesses _____ (____to____) (____to____) (____to____) (____to____) (____to____) (____to____)

Presiding Member(s)

Chairman Ted Poe

Check all of the following that apply:

Open Session ☑   Electronically Recorded (taped) ☑
Executive (closed) Session ☐   Stenographic Record ☑
Televised ☑

TITLE OF HEARING:

Evaluating the Export-Import Bank in the Global Economy

SUBCOMMITTEE MEMBERS PRESENT:

Reps. Poe, Keating, Sherman, Perry, Castro

NON-SUBCOMMITTEE MEMBERS PRESENT: *(Mark with an * if they are not members of full committee.)*

Reps. Rohrabacher, Moore*, Heck*

HEARING WITNESSES: Same as meeting notice attached? Yes ☑ No ☐
(If "no", please list below and include title, agency, department, or organization.)

STATEMENTS FOR THE RECORD: *(List any statements submitted for the record.)*

SFRs submitted by Rep. Poe on behalf of: U.S. Chamber of Commerce, Nate LaMar (Draper Inc.), Don Nelson (ProGauge Technologies Inc.), Steve Wilburn (FirmGreen Inc.), Linda Menghetti Dempsey (National Association of Manufacturers), Diane Katz (Heritage Foundation)

TIME SCHEDULED TO RECONVENE _____
or
TIME ADJOURNED ___*10:52 a.m.*___

_____
Subcommittee Staff Director

MATERIAL SUBMITTED FOR THE RECORD BY THE HONORABLE TED POE, A REPRESENTA-
TIVE IN CONGRESS FROM THE STATE OF TEXAS, AND CHAIRMAN, SUBCOMMITTEE ON
TERRORISM, NONPROLIFERATION, AND TRADE

CHAMBER OF COMMERCE
OF THE
UNITED STATES OF AMERICA

R. BRUCE JOSTEN
EXECUTIVE VICE PRESIDENT
GOVERNMENT AFFAIRS

1615 H STREET, N.W.
WASHINGTON, D.C. 20062-2000
202/463-5310

October 22, 2015

The Honorable Ted Poe
Chairman
Subcommittee on Terrorism, Nonproliferation
   and Trade
Committee on Foreign Affairs
U.S. House of Representatives
Washington, DC 20515

The Honorable William Keating
Ranking Member
Subcommittee on Terrorism, Nonproliferation
   and Trade
Committee on Foreign Affairs
U.S. House of Representatives
Washington, DC 20515

Dear Chairman Poe and Ranking Member Keating:

The U.S. Chamber of Commerce is pleased to provide the following comments in
advance of the hearing of the House Foreign Affairs Subcommittee on Terrorism,
Nonproliferation, and Trade entitled "Evaluating the Export-Import Bank in the Global
Economy." The U.S. Chamber is the world's largest business federation, representing the
interests of more than three million businesses of all sizes, sectors, and regions, as well as state
and local chambers and industry associations, and dedicated to promoting, protecting, and
defending America's free enterprise system.

On behalf of the hundreds of thousands of small and medium-sized companies in our
national federation, the Chamber urges Congress to approve legislation to reauthorize and reform
the U.S. Export-Import Bank (Ex-Im) as expeditiously as possible.

Ex-Im is a vital part of the American economy. Ex-Im has supported more than 150,000
American jobs at 3,000 companies that depend on the Bank's services in order to compete in
global markets. Failure to reauthorize Ex-Im has put at risk hundreds of thousands of American
jobs and damaged many small- and medium-sized businesses. Without the Bank's services,
American companies lack crucial support overseas and fall behind foreign competitors.

Below, please find statements from more than 80 small- and medium-size businesses
from all across the country on the importance of Ex-Im. To read their stories in full, please visit
our website: www.uschamber.com/ex-im.

Thank you for your consideration of these views.

Sincerely,

R. Bruce Josten

cc: Members of the Subcommittee on Terrorism, Nonproliferation, and Trade

Testimony: Nate LaMar, Draper Inc.
House Foreign Affairs Subcommittee Hearing
"Evaluating the Export-Import Bank in the Global Economy"

My name is Nate LaMar. I'm the International Regional Manager at Draper Inc., I serve on the Indiana District Export Council, and am President of Henry County Council. Having graduated from West Point, I now serve as Military Academy Liaison Officer for Indiana's 6th Congressional District.

I'm grateful for the opportunity to share the story of how my employer benefits from Ex-Im, and how much is at stake if Ex-Im remains closed for not only my employer, but for over one hundred other Indiana businesses.

Indiana is the most manufacturing-intensive state in the country. In Indiana, Ex-Im supported over 1.8 billion in export sales from 2007-2014. In that period, it supported 12,000 jobs at 130 Indiana companies. My employer, Draper Inc., is just one of them.

Draper Inc. is a manufacturer and is the largest private sector employer in Henry County, Indiana. We employ 500 people, and since our inception in 1902, we've never laid off a single employee.

We started as a window shade manufacturer, but today we also produce projection screens, projector lifts, solar control coverings, and gym equipment. In a time when manufacturing is on the decline, we're very proud to be doing our part to keep the Made In the USA brand alive.

Back in 2007, we were working with J&S Mexico. Even though credit was tight, through Ex-Im financing, we were able to sell $50,000 of audiovisual equipment to J&S. In a world without Ex-Im, that contract would have gone to a foreign enterprise that enjoys the backing of its own national export credit agencies. I know that without Ex-Im, many of our overseas clients would not do business with Draper.

I travel abroad extensively for business, and I know first-hand that the global economy is only getting more competitive. U.S. job creators need to use every tool in their arsenals to create good-paying jobs at home by selling goods abroad. Ex-Im is essential to that process.

This summer alone, China devalued its currency, India's largest airline made a $27 billion dollar purchase of 250 Airbus aircraft, and the stock market suffered a one-day three percent drop. All three of these disparate events could have been better for U.S. jobs, if Americans could more easily export our products abroad.

I'm thankful my Senators, Dan Coats and Joe Donnelly, voted with the majority of the U.S. Senate to revive Ex-Im in late July before the summer Congressional recess. I'm also glad that Indiana Representatives Larry Bucshon and Andre Carson signed the discharge petition to bring Ex-Im to a fair vote in the House.

I urge Congress to reauthorize Ex-Im as soon as possible so that companies like Draper can continue to hire and grow.

Testimony: Don Nelson, ProGauge Technologies Inc.

House Foreign Affairs Subcommittee Hearing
"Evaluating the Export-Import Bank in the Global Economy"

I'm Don Nelson, and I'm chief executive of ProGauge Technologies Inc. in Bakersfield California. We're a manufacturer of oil industry equipment like steam generators and metering equipment, and have been selling our wares domestically since 1998 and abroad with the help of the Export-Import Bank since 2006.

I'm grateful for this opportunity to share our story, because if Ex-Im isn't reauthorized, our ability to export will be seriously jeopardized. Exports are vital for my company, which I'll explain further, but since the topic of this hearing is the role of Ex-Im in the global economy, I'd like to first talk about why America needs Ex-Im in the international market.

Exports are the key to keeping the U.S. competitive on a global scale in so many ways. It's simple: Exports help us establish strategic relationships in foreign countries. They help U.S. companies stay in the game at a time when the international economy is getting more and more competitive.

China's not eliminating its export credit agency. In fact, it's increasing support for Chinese exporters, which begs the question: why would the United States be the only country to cut these resources? Why do we want to hand over any advantage we have, or relationships we've built, to other countries?

For ProGauge, Ex-Im means putting our equipment in oil fields all over the world. Exports make up over 65 percent of our revenue. Without Ex-Im, we just won't have enough collateral to work on our projects, and for our 60 employees, that kind of uncertainty is very troubling.

Right now, we've submitted a bid for a multiyear project in the Middle East worth up to $40 million. Winning this project would offset a slowdown at ProGauge, but without Ex-Im, we wouldn't be able to provide the guarantee necessary for the buyer. So we had to get creative. We decided to subcontract to a fabricator to build the equipment in the Middle East, which will allow us to do the project without a bank guarantee.

The downside of doing this project without Ex-Im is that the majority of jobs will be created in the Middle East, not the U.S. I estimate that about 30-40 jobs will be created from this project. But only 5-10 will be in the U.S., and the rest will be in the Middle East. We don't know yet if we won the project, but we will know soon.

Exports mean jobs, and Congress needs to act accordingly. As long as Ex-Im remains closed, jobs are at risk. The jobs from that project could have be planned for the U.S. if Ex-Im was available.

These consequences are too much for small businesses, which are the lifeblood of the U.S. economy. Congress needs to stand with workers and reauthorize Ex-Im now. On the global stage and in my shop in Bakersfield, the stakes are too high to wait any longer.

––––––––

Testimony: Steve Wilburn, CEO FirmGreen Inc.
House Foreign Affairs Subcommittee Hearing
"Evaluating the Export-Import Bank in the Global Economy"

My name is Steve Wilburn. I'm a Veteran of the Vietnam War, a Marine, and a proud American businessman. I'm the CEO of FirmGreen Inc. in Newport Beach, California, and I depend on the Ex-Im Bank to conduct my business.

FirmGreen is a leader in alternative energy. We convert resources like landfill gas into renewable energy and clean fuel. We also have patented battery storage technology for renewable energy generation, the VerdeVault™. Many international companies are interested in utilizing clean energy, and we use the Ex-Im Bank to take advantage of that overseas demand.

In 2012, we used the Ex-Im Bank to secure a project that developed clean fuel from landfills in Brazil, which generated 165 new manufacturing jobs across seven states. If I were to try to bid for that project today, I wouldn't have the financing most countries require, and a foreign firm would probably win the contract.

Those are the stakes for exporters: by taking away Ex-Im, you're taking away their seat at the table on countless international projects.

That's why it's fitting that this hearing is entitled "Evaluating the Export-Import Bank in the Global Economy." From my vantage point, Ex-Im is essential to not only level the playing field globally, but to keep the U.S. in the fight.

Our foreign competitors have their governments in their corner. China's ramping up support for its export credit agency, and countries like the U.K., Canada, and Brazil have strong credit agencies as well. Why should we unilaterally disarm when other countries are leading the charge to export and grow their influence? Ex-Im was a key tool in keeping U.S. exporters and suppliers competitive, but since its lapse, the consequences have been dire.

To many Members of Congress, I'm no stranger. I've come to Washington three times on my own dime to try to reason with Congress to support Ex-Im. That's because so much is on the line for FirmGreen and thousands of other small and medium-sized businesses across the country.

Opponents of the Bank keep saying that Ex-Im isn't the lender of last resort. They say that businesses like mine have alternative sources of financing. Well, to any Member of Congress who has suggested that company seek private financing during Ex-Im's lapse, I'd like to ask a question: Where are these alternate sources? I'd love to use them.

But the truth is, that claim isn't rooted in reality. Suppliers and exporters know their needs better than anyone else. And when jobs and growth are on the line, Congress should listen.

Ex-Im supports growth at home by helping manufacturers export abroad. Reauthorization should be a top priority for any Member who supports U.S. jobs. I urge Congress to reauthorize Ex-Im as soon as possible.

Leading Innovation. Creating Opportunity. Pursuing Progress.

Statement for the Record

of Linda Menghetti Dempsey
Vice President, International Economic Affairs
National Association of Manufacturers

For the Hearing of the House Financial Services Committee
Subcommittee on Terrorism, Nonproliferation and Trade

on "Evaluating the Export-Import Bank in the Global Economy"

October 23, 2015

Statement for Record by
Linda Menghetti Dempsey

Vice President, International Economic Affairs
National Association of Manufacturers

For the

Hearing of the House Foreign Affairs Committee
Subcommittee on Terrorism, Nonproliferation, and Trade

on "Evaluating the Export-Import Bank in the Global Economy"

October 23, 2015

I appreciate the chance to highlight on behalf of the National Association of Manufacturers (NAM) the importance of reauthorizing the U.S. Export-Import Bank to help manufacturers compete in the global marketplace that will enable them to support and sustain good-paying manufacturing jobs throughout every state.

The NAM is the nation's largest industrial association and voice for more than 12 million women and men who make things in America. Manufacturing in the U.S. supports more than 17 million jobs, and in 2014, U.S. manufacturing output reached a record of nearly $2.1 trillion. It is the engine that drives the U.S. economy by creating jobs, opportunity and prosperity. The NAM is committed to achieving a policy agenda that helps manufacturers grow and create jobs. Manufacturing has the biggest multiplier effect of any industry and manufacturers in the United States perform more than three-quarters of all private-sector R&D in the nation – driving more innovation than any other sector.

<u>Importance of Exports to U.S. Manufacturing and Jobs</u>

Since its origin, the United States has recognized the importance of exports to promoting industrial and economic growth and supporting jobs. The ability of U.S. companies to export has also been a critical issue for the NAM since its founding. With 95 percent of consumers outside the United States and global demand for manufactured goods that far exceeds domestic demand, manufacturers in the United States need to win more sales overseas if they are going to sustain and grow operations and employment.

World trade in manufactured goods reached $11.8 trillion in 2013[1] and greatly exceeds U.S. consumption of manufactured goods (domestic shipments and imports), which totaled $4.1 trillion in 2014. U.S. manufactured goods exports have more than doubled in the past decade, reaching a record $1.6 trillion in 2014. While that growth is impressive, U.S. manufacturers and exporters are facing an increasingly challenging global economy where growth has slowed. America lags behind many of its largest trading partners when it comes to exporting. U.S. exports comprised only 9.5 percent of global trade in manufactured goods in 2013. We can and

---

[1] Data from the World Trade Organization Statistical Database, accessed on Jan. 29, 2015. Most recent data available.

must do more to expand U.S. exports if we are going to grow manufacturing and the jobs it supports in the United States.

The importance of exports to the bottom line for manufacturers across the United States is not a theoretical issue. More than 40 percent of respondents in a recent National Association of Manufacturers (NAM) survey cited exports as a primary driver of growth for their company.[2] Those survey respondents who were more positive about their export potential over the next 12 months were also more optimistic in their company's economic outlook, sales and capital spending plans.

Nor are exports a theoretical issue for the workers employed in every state by our nation's manufacturers. As new export opportunities emerge overseas, manufacturers in the United States are able to both sustain and create American jobs. According to the latest figures from the U.S. Department of Commerce, every $1 billion in exports creates or supports 5,796 jobs.

Recently, exports have played a significant role in the ongoing manufacturing recovery. Since the end of 2009, export-intensive sectors with substantial export growth have seen the largest job gains. U.S. exports accounted for about one-third of GDP growth from 2009 to 2014, but the current macroeconomic environment poses serious risks for manufacturers and manufacturing exporters. Additionally, jobs supported by exports pay on average 18 percent more than other jobs.[3] Employees in the "most trade-intensive industries" earn an average compensation of nearly $94,000, or more than 56 percent more than those in manufacturing companies that were less engaged in trade.[4]

Importance of Ex-Im Bank to Growing U.S. Exports

One vital tool that thousands of manufacturers use to compete successfully in global markets is the Ex-Im Bank. The NAM strongly supports Ex-Im Bank's mission to support U.S. jobs through exports and views the Bank as one of the most important tools the U.S. government has to help grow U.S. exports and jobs.

The Export-Import Bank is essential to boosting exports of U.S. products. In FY2014, Ex-Im Bank enabled more than $27 billion in exports – leveraging about $20.5 billion in authorizations. Nearly 90 percent of those transactions directly supported small-businesses, with an estimated $5 billion in support for small business exporters. Furthermore, the Bank has maintained its incredibly low default rate of through the recession and through several years of record growth. At the end of FY2014, the Bank's default rate was less 0.2 percent. Notably, Ex-Im's activities are already targeted and, by law, must not compete with private sector lending activity.

[2] Moutray, Chad, "NAM/IndustryWeek Survey: Manufacturers Bullish, But Frustrated with Washington," IndustryWeek, June 9, 2014. See http://www.industryweek.com/global-economy/namindustryweek-survey-manufacturers-bullish-frustrated-washington?page=1.
[3] David Riker, Do Jobs in Export Industries Still Pay More? And Why?, International Trade Administration, U.S. Department of Commerce, July 2010, accessed at www.trade.gov/mas/ian/build/groups/public/@tg_ian/documents/webcontent/tg_ian_003208.pdf.
[4] Calculations from the Manufacturers Alliance for Productivity and Innovation (MAPI) Foundation, using 2013 input-output data from the Bureau of Economic Analysis, accessed at www.themanufacturinginstitute.org/Research/Facts-About-Manufacturing/Foreign-Trade-and-Investment/Impact-on-Compensation/Impact-on-Compensation.aspx.

Ex-Im Bank helped promote just under two percent of total U.S. exports in FY2014. While it does not need to finance the great majority of U.S. exports, it is considered vital in certain areas of significant growth, particularly for small- and medium-sized business exporters, long-term financing for large projects, sales to emerging markets and sales to foreign state-owned entities.

- Small and Medium-Sized Business Exports. Ex-Im is vital to many and medium-sized businesses to enable them to start to export overseas. Small businesses, both those that are direct exporters and those that supply domestically to larger U.S. exporters, will feel the blow if Congress fails to reauthorize Ex-Im Bank. Those companies that utilize Ex-Im Bank insurance programs to enable their working capital will be faced almost immediately with a dilemma about how to pay their workers and make the mortgage payments on their facilities, let alone consider growing and hiring. Suppliers whose U.S. customers lose out on large infrastructure, aerospace and energy projects overseas because they cannot bid without access to Ex-Im Bank will also see their orders shrink. Of the Bank's 3,300 small business transactions in FY 2014, 545 companies were first-time Ex-Im users. Ex-Im's role in jump-starting new small and medium-sized exporters is particularly important.

  Many small and medium-sized manufacturers across the country have turned to Ex-Im Bank to take advantage of new international trade opportunities and grow their workforce. Special Products & Mfg., Inc. (SPM) in Rockwall, Texas, is a second-generation, family-owned business that has grown – with the help of exports – from a small garage shop in the 1960s into a firm with more than 200 machine operators, welders, assemblers, engineers and other associates in a 140,000 square foot state-of-the-art factory. Over the past several years, SPM has seized opportunities to expand their business into the world marketplace. From Europe to South America, SPM is exporting products ranging from new and improved gas station pumps to large steel enclosures for drill rig drives. SPM also supplies many companies like General Electric and Caterpillar, and SPM's Chief Operator Officer Ed Grand-Lienard made the trip to Washington earlier this year to let Congress know that the future of American manufacturing is in jeopardy of being seriously hurt if the Ex-Im Bank is not reauthorized. This company is just one of the many small businesses that have reaped the benefits of expanded market access and tools like Ex-Im Bank, and the NAM would be happy to provide others to the committee.

- *Long-Term Project Finance.* Ex-Im Bank, like foreign export credit agencies (ECAs), has taken on an increasingly important facilitation role for export financing as the role of commercial banks in financing long-term projects continues to shrink in the wake of the financial crisis. U.S. regulatory guidelines that favor domestic receivables over foreign sales[5], implementation of Basel III rules[6] and the European sovereign debt crisis[7] have all impacted the ability and appetite of banks to participate in long-term export financing projects at competitive rates. While some banks have been able to restore effectively their balance sheets, commercial bank participation in long-term, high-volume funding (tenors longer than 10 years and over a few hundred million

---

[5] Office of the Comptroller of the Currency, Treasury Department, Comptroller's Handbook, at 17-18, accessed at http://www.occ.gov/publications/publications-by-type/comptrollers-handbook/pub-ch-asset-based-lending.pdf.
[6] Basel Committee on Banking Supervision, "Basel III: A global regulatory framework for more resilient banks and banking systems." December 2010, accessed at http://www.bis.org/publ/bcbs189.pdf.
[7] Berne Union Yearbook 2012 at 55, accessed at http://www.berneunion.org/wp-content/uploads/2013/10/Berne-Union-Yearbook-2012.pdf - Quoting Steve Tvardek, Head of the OECD Export Credits Division, OECD.

dollars) remains highly selective. Many experts – including top executives from UK Export Finance (UKEF), Korea Trade Insurance Corporation (K-Sure) and Deutsche Bank – suggest that Basel III will continue to constrain commercial banks from playing a significant role as long-term funders of large-scale projects and other sales.[8] As a result, ECAs are increasingly a driving force for large-scale, long-term projects – particularly projects in the infrastructure, energy and aerospace sectors.[9] *Infrastructure Journal* data show that ECA lending activity in commercial project finance transactions increased threefold from less than $10 billion in 2009 to more than $30 billion projected for 2013, and ECAs are providing the only project finance available in some markets. In particular, Japan Bank for International Cooperation (JBIC) is a global leader for energy and infrastructure project finance[10] and Korea EximBank is rising in prominence, particularly in its priority energy sector.[11]

- *Emerging Markets*. Many U.S.-based lenders also turn to Ex-Im to mitigate geopolitical and collateral risk in an effort to provide viable trade financing solutions for exporters. Without Ex-Im, many private lenders have limited options: opt not to finance otherwise viable export activity in emerging markets, charge rates that are uncompetitive globally or place limits on the overall amount of financing to particular emerging markets. Ex-Im Bank, for example, offers medium- and long-term guarantees that provide flexible lender financing options for buyers of U.S. capital goods and services. Ex-Im also supports commercial banks through letter of credit (LC) confirmations that reduce a bank's risks, offering private sector lenders greater flexibility in working with their client base.

- *Government and State-Owned Enterprise (SOE) Transactions*. U.S. exporters from a broad number of sectors increasingly are selling to foreign governments and state-owned entities. Be it medical equipment sales to foreign state-owned hospitals, power generation equipment to foreign state-owned utilities or communications satellites to foreign governments for national mobile satellite systems, such sales support greater exports and jobs in the United States, but are difficult to win. In some cases, the foreign purchaser favors suppliers with a government entity on the other side of the table. In other cases, like a nuclear power plant project overseas, an ECA lending option is a requirement to participate in the initial bidding phase – even if the customer ultimately opts for another financing option. While the governments of most of the United States' major trading partners are willing to oblige, Ex-Im is the only government entity able to play such a role for U.S. exporters. Without Ex-Im's presence, U.S. exporters simply would not be eligible to compete for many of these substantial foreign sales.

In short, while Ex-Im's role is relatively small compared to the overall size of U.S. exports, it plays an outsized and highly important role in opening the door to U.S. exports for

---

[8] Berne Union Yearbook 2014 at 66, accessed at http://www.berneunion.org/wp-content/uploads/2012/10/Berne-Union-80-Yearbook-2014.pdf.

[9] *See, e.g.*, "Power Shift: The Rise of Export Credit and Development Finance in Major Projects." November 2013; Baker & McKenzie with Infrastructure Journal, accessed at
http://www.bakermckenzie.com/files/Publication/7dc07b54-651f-4168-9c81-0abdfdc432ca/Presentation/PublicationAttachment/6943f6ae-5718-42f8-a587-9a06c65902d7/fc_global_powershift_nov13.pdf.

[10] "Power Shift: The Rise of Export Credit and Development Finance in Major Projects." [need Publication, date]

[11] "Filling the funding gap – Korea Eximbank" Project Finance International (March 2013), accessed at http://www.pfie.com/filling-the-funding-gap-%E2%80%93-korea-eximbank/21071929.article.

certain types of transactions where U.S. exporters continue to see substantial growth opportunities.

The Global Export Credit Dimension

One of the significant roles that the Ex-Im Bank plays is aiding U.S. exporters and their workers to compete in a global economy that is characterized by dramatically increasing export credit assistance provided by governments in Europe, Asia and Latin America. As detailed in a study released by the NAM in 2014, *The Global Export Credit Dimension: The Size of Foreign Export Credit Agencies Compared to the United States* (2014),[12] the ECAs of our top nine trading partners – Brazil, Canada, China, France, Germany, Japan, Mexico, South Korea and the United Kingdom – provided nearly half a trillion dollars in annual export support. Other key findings of that report include:

- The ECAs of China, Japan, South Korea and Germany are already individually larger than the Ex-Im Bank, and all of the nine major foreign ECAs are larger as a share of their countries' GDP than the Ex-Im Bank is compared to U.S. GDP;
- China's primary ECA provides more than five times the assistance than the U.S. Ex-Im Bank does;
- Major foreign ECAs, including those in Germany, China and Canada, are expanding exports more successfully than the Ex-Im Bank. The Ex-Im Bank supported 2.42 percent of total U.S. exports in 2013, while Germany (3.63 percent), China (12.50 percent) and Canada (20.29 percent) helped to support even more international sales;
- Foreign ECA activity grew sharply in several major countries, including China, South Korea and Canada, between 2005 and 2013; and
- Official ECA activity is particularly critical to key and growing manufacturing sectors of the global economy, including infrastructure and transportation where manufacturers in the United States are well positioned to grow in related exports if competitive financing is available.

While the United States is a relatively small player in ECA activity, it has worked intensively to negotiate strong rules to eliminate market distortions and subsidies that oftentimes characterize foreign ECAs. In particular, the United States has led efforts to bring developed country members of the Organization for Economic Cooperation and Development (OECD)[13] and non-OECD countries to the negotiating table. Largely as a result of U.S. leadership over several decades, most of the OECD's industrialized countries have agreed to uniform standards for fair and commercially based ECA lending.[14] Sector-specific arrangements have also been

---

[12] NAM, *The Global Export Credit Dimension: The Size of Foreign Export Credit Agencies Compared to the United States* (2014), accessed at
http://www.nam.org/uploadedFiles/NAM/Site_Content/Issues/Global%20Export%20Credit%20Dimension%20Web.pdf; see also NAM, *Forfeiting Opportunity: Ex-Im Bank Reauthorization Is Essential for Manufacturers to Compete Globally in the Face of Massive Foreign Export Credit Financing* (2014), accessed at
http://www.nam.org/uploadedFiles/NAM/Site_Content/Issues/Forfeiting%20Opportunity%20Web.pdf.
[13] Members include Australia, Austria, Belgium, Canada, Chile, Czech Republic, Denmark, Estonia, Finland, France, Germany, Greece, Hungary, Iceland, Ireland, Israel, Italy, Japan, Luxembourg, Mexico, Netherlands, New Zealand, Norway, Poland, Portugal, Slovak Republic, Slovenia, South Korea, Spain, Sweden, Switzerland, Turkey, United Kingdom and United States. OECD, "Members and Partners," accessed at
http://www.oecd.org/about/membersandpartners/.
[14] Most prominently, OECD members developed the "Arrangement on Officially Supported Export Credits" (ECA Arrangement) that sets out financial disciplines for standard export credits and for export credits for certain sectors that reduce and eliminate potential market distortions. In particular, the ECA Arrangement – which has been agreed

negotiated to provide even stricter discipline on ECA financing related to ships, nuclear power, aircraft, renewable energy, climate change mitigation and water projects.[15]

Work with non-OECD countries has been more difficult and that is where the greatest concern about subsidized ECA financing lies. The United States has worked intensively to undertake negotiations with key developing countries to agree to operate their ECAs based only on commercial considerations. As a result of U.S. efforts, 18 major providers of export credits[16] have been invited to participate in the International Working Group on Export Credits (IWG), which held its first meeting in November 2012 and has met several times. Work is slow as many non-OECD participants have been "cautious" and not clearly committed to the process.[17]

The U.S. Ex-Im Bank's role, while small in the global economy, is critical to many thousands of exporters. Failing to reauthorize Ex-Im is tantamount to unilateral disarmament and will also negate U.S. leadership in seeking to eliminate foreign ECA market distortions and subsidies.

Ex-Im Lapse Hurting U.S. Manufacturers

This week, the NAM released new analysis about the impact to manufacturers since the charter of the U.S. Export-Import (Ex-Im) Bank expired on June 30. The expiration of the Ex-Im Bank's charter on June 30 has left several thousand manufacturers, many of them small and medium-sized exporters, without adequate access to capital and the financing they need to compete with foreign manufacturers. Orbital ATK, for example, recently lost a bid to sell a satellite to Azerbaijan because the customer identified Ex-Im Bank financing as a "must-have." International Green Structures, a small business with a manufacturing facility in Texas, has a significant deal to sell its sustainable shelters in Kenya stuck in a holding pattern until Ex-Im Bank's charter is renewed.

There are 83 official export credit agencies across the globe, many of which continue to close on deals worth tens of billions of dollars. The Ex-Im's lapse has created a credit and liquidity crunch for small and medium-sized businesses. The NAM white paper estimates that more than 500 U.S. exporters will lose their credit insurance policies between September 1 and December 1 this year, meaning that they will be unable to insure their foreign receivables and acquire financing for new exporters. Additionally, users of Ex-Im's multi-buyer credit insurance cannot add new foreign customers to their policies, thereby reducing their opportunities to expand in overseas markets.

---

to by Australia, Canada, the European Union, Japan, New Zealand, Norway, South Korea, Switzerland and the United States, emphasizes that OECD ECAs should be competing "on quality and price of goods and services exported rather than on the most favourable officially supported terms." OECD, "Official Export Credit Agencies," accessed at http://www.oecd.org/tad/xcred/eca.htm; see also, OECD, *"Official Export Credit Agencies,"* accessed at http://www.oecd.org/tad/xcred/eca.htm.

[15] OECD, "Official Export Credit Agencies," accessed at http://www.oecd.org/tad/xcred/eca.htm.

[16] The 18 participants are nine participants in the OECD arrangement (Australia, Canada, the European Union, Japan, New Zealand, South Korea, Switzerland United States) and nine non-OECD members (Brazil, China, India, Indonesia, Israel, Malaysia, Russian Federation, South Africa and Turkey).

[17] "Report on Export Credit Negotiations," U.S. Department of the Treasury, December 2013. The IWG held two full meetings (hosted by China in May 2013 and the European Union in September 2013) and one technical meeting (hosted by Germany in March 2013); European Commission, Report from the Commission to the European Parliament and the Council – Annual Report on negotiations undertaken by the Commission in the field of export credits, in the sense of Regulation (EU) No 1233/2011 (May 28, 2014), accessed at http://eur-lex.europa.eu/legal-content/EN/TXT/?uri=COM:2014:299:FIN.

Manufacturers need Congress to act quickly on legislation to provide a long-term reauthorization of Ex-Im Bank. Reliable access to export financing is a vital part of being globally competitive, and the Ex-Im Bank has taken on even greater significance in today's turbulent financial environment. Manufacturers in the United States – and their customers overseas – operate based on long-term plans that often involve multiyear projects in which the Ex-Im Bank is a critical partner. Without the certainty of a long-term Ex-Im reauthorization, U.S. exporters have already been put at a significant disadvantage, which will hamper growth here at home and result in lost opportunities for American workers and businesses.

If Congress fails to act quickly a long-term reauthorization of Ex-Im Bank, manufacturers will continue to forfeit opportunities to competitors overseas and, thereby, risk the loss not just of exports but of manufacturing growth and good-paying jobs in every state.

Weakening America's export competitiveness will be particularly damaging in the face of intense and growing global competition that has already resulted in a substantial decline in America's share of the global manufacturing market. Even greater manufacturing export opportunities will be lost on an annual basis as trade expands and U.S. exporters effectively cede foreign sales. The loss of new export opportunities will be particularly severe for small- and medium-sized businesses and for exports to emerging markets and infrastructure sectors where growth is expected to be strongest.

Time is of the essence. The lapse in the Bank's charter is putting ever more U.S. export sales as risk.

Conclusion

There is broad support for Ex-Im Bank's reauthorization from job-creators across the country. The Ex-Im Bank is a targeted tool and a last resort that enables U.S. businesses to find a foothold in an increasingly competitive marketplace. The failure to reauthorize the Ex-Im Bank has already had lasting and damaging effects on manufacturers of every size throughout out the United States, threatening tens of billions of dollars in export sales as well as the security of hundreds of thousands of American jobs that depend directly or indirectly on the Ex-Im Bank's export financing. I urge Congress to consider the vital role that ECAs play in the global marketplace and to move forward quickly on a long-term reauthorization for Ex-Im Bank to enable it to effectively fulfill its principal mission of supporting U.S. jobs through exports.

———

The **Heritage Foundation**

ISSUE BRIEF

No. 4355 | FEBRUARY 24, 2015

Export-Import Bank Impervious to Reform
Diane Katz

Despite overwhelming evidence to the contrary, some Members of Congress believe that a few legislative tweaks will remedy all that is wrong with the Export-Import Bank (Ex-Im).[1] In fact, the pending House bill to reauthorize Ex-Im through 2019 is largely a regurgitation of "reforms" previously mandated by Congress—without appreciable effect. The only meaningful way to remedy Ex-Im's multibillion-dollar risk to taxpayers—and the rampant cronyism the export subsidies perpetrate—is to allow the bank's charter to expire.

Existing law provides for an orderly shutdown of Ex-Im if Congress does not renew the charter by June 30.[2] All existing financing would remain in effect until the contractual expiration dates.

Opposition to reauthorization is mounting as legislators and the public become more aware of the bank's mismanagement, dysfunction, and risk, all of which has repeatedly been documented by the Office of Inspector General[3] and the Government Accountability Office.[4] Nonetheless, legislation introduced on January 28 by Representative Stephen Fincher (R–TN) would reauthorize the Ex-Im charter through 2019 and mandate changes in some bank procedures.[5]

Bank procedures certainly could be improved, but Ex-Im officials have thwarted past attempts by Congress to impose reforms. More important, no amount of bureaucratic tinkering can shield taxpayers from bailouts[6] in the event that bank reserves run dry—as occurred in the 1980s—nor will it protect American businesses from the disadvantages of the U.S. government subsidizing their foreign competitors.[7] The *only* remedy for Ex-Im's worst consequences is to shut it down.

Fincher makes much of the fact that he has garnered 57 co-sponsors for his bill.[8] But the support of these Members actually demonstrates the very cronyism that needs to be ended. Ending such cronyism would be a step toward achieving opportunity for all and favoritism for none.[9]

For example, Representative Aaron Schock (R–IL) claims to oppose government subsidies—with the exception of the $1.6 billion in subsidized Ex-Im financing that benefitted the Caterpillar, Inc., operations in his district between 2010 and 2014.[10] (The company is the world's leading manufacturer of construction and mining equipment, with a market cap of nearly $52 billion.)

Schock's district also includes Komatsu American Corp., a U.S. subsidiary of a Japanese conglomerate with annual revenues exceeding $55 billion. This, the world's second-largest manufacturer and supplier of earth-moving equipment, benefitted from Ex-Im financing in excess of $460 million in 2013 alone.

Representative Glenn Thompson (R–PA) also a co-sponsor, recently pledged to "support stronger economic growth and upward mobility for individuals and families."[11] But the economics literature is virtually unanimous in finding that subsidies, in general, and export subsidies, in particular, are detrimental to the economy. Thompson's dis-

This paper, in its entirely, can be found at
http://report.heritage.org/ib4355

The Heritage Foundation
214 Massachusetts Avenue, NE
Washington, DC 20002
(202) 546-4400 | heritage.org

ISSUE BRIEF | NO. 4355
FEBRUARY 24, 2015

trict includes General Electric International, which has benefitted from more than $5 billion in Ex-Im financing since 2007.

Co-sponsor Tom Cole (R–OK) argues that Ex-Im is necessary for allowing small business to grow[12]—even though the bank serves just 0.5 percent of small businesses nationwide. Cole's district includes Halliburton Energy Services, a subsidiary of the oil-drilling giant, which benefited from more than $1.1 billion in subsidized Ex-Im financing in 2008 and 2010 combined.

Each of these examples, along with the multitude of other Ex-Im subsidies for mega-corporations, belies advocates' claims that Ex-Im is a necessity. As it is, the bank finances less than 2 percent of total U.S. exports (by value). The recent record levels of American exports indicate no shortage of private financing.

Fincher states that Ex-Im is "in dire need of major reforms."[13] Changes to bank procedures might have marginal effects on the mismanagement noted in a variety of audits, but there is no reform that would prevent the economic distortions caused by Ex-Im's subsidized financing.[14] Most every government subsidy produces disparity elsewhere in the economy. In the case of Ex-Im, the losers include domestic companies that are left to compete against foreign firms and foreign governments bankrolled by U.S. taxpayers.

Many provisions in the Fincher bill (H.R. 597) duplicate existing policies. Following are descriptions of the major elements in the legislation compared to current policy.

Risk

H.R. 597: The bill calls for the appointment of a chief risk officer tasked to work with Ex-Im's board of directors' Audit Committee to develop, implement, and manage processes to reduce risks to the bank portfolio, which currently totals more than $140 billion. The bill directs the Office of Inspector General to audit the risk-management procedures. (Curiously, the legislation also increases risk by dra-

1. The bank funnels billions of taxpayer dollars each year to overseas businesses for the purchase of American products.

2. Congress agreed to a short-term, nine-month Ex-Im reauthorization last fall when the measure was tied to a stopgap spending bill to avert a government shutdown.

3. Diane Katz, "Mismanagement of Export-Import Bank Invites Fraud," Heritage Foundation testimony, July 29, 2014, http://www.heritage.org/research/testimony/2014/08/mismanagement-of-export-import-bank-invites-fraud.

4. Diane Katz, "The Export-Import Bank: A Government Outfit Mired in Mismanagement," Heritage Foundation *Issue Brief* No. 4208, April 29, 2014, http://thf_media.s3.amazonaws.com/2014/pdf/IB4208.pdf.

5. H.R. 597, The Reform Exports and Expand the American Economy Act, 114th Congress.

6. Diane Katz, "Oops. The Export-Import Bank Is Actually Losing Taxpayer Money," The Daily Signal, May 22, 2014, http://dailysignal.com/2014/05/22/export-import-bank-actually-losing-taxpayer-money/.

7. Daniel J. Ikenson, "The Export-Import Bank and Its Victims: Which Industries and States Bear the Brunt?" Cato Institute *Policy Analysis* No. 756, September 10, 2004, http://www.cato.org/publications/policy-analysis/export-import-bank-its-victims-which-industries-states-bear-brunt (accessed February 20, 2015).

8. News release, "58 Members of Congress Support Ex-Im Reform Legislation," U.S. Representative Stephen Fincher, January 28, 2015, http://fincher.house.gov/media-center/press-releases/58-members-of-congress-support-ex-im-reform-legislation (accessed February 20, 2015).

9. Heritage Action for America, "Opportunity for All, Favoritism to None," http://heritageaction.com/opportunityforall/.

10. "Schock Criticizes Government Subsidies But Supports Export-Import Bank," *Illinois Review*, video, August 7, 2014, http://illinoisreview.typepad.com/illinoisreview/2014/08/schock-criticizes-government-subsidies-but-supports-export-import-bank.html (accessed February 20, 2015).

11. News release, "Thompson Sworn In to 114th Congress, Discusses Legislative & Committee Priorities," Congressman Glen "GT" Thompson," January 6, 2015, http://thompson.house.gov/press-release/thompson-sworn-114th-congress-discusses-legislative-committee-priorities (accessed February 20, 2015).

12. Tom Cole, "Ex-Im Bank Benefits American Economy," *The Journal Record*, September 22, 2014, http://journalrecord.com/2014/09/22/cole-ex-im-bank-benefits-american-economy-opinion/#ix773E97AfC50 (accessed February 20, 2015)

13. News release, "58 Members of Congress Support Ex-Im Reform Legislation."

14. Veronique de Rugy, "The Unseen Costs of the Export-Import Bank," *U.S. News & World Report*, July 7, 2014, http://www.usnews.com/opinion/economic-intelligence/2014/07/07/export-import-bank-hurts-businesses-and-taxpayers (accessed February 20, 2015).

ISSUE BRIEF | NO. 4355
FEBRUARY 24, 2015

matically expanding the authority of Ex-Im advisors to unilaterally approve applications for loans, credit guarantees, and insurance.)

Current Policy: Bank officials hired a chief risk officer in 2013, and established an Enterprise Risk Committee in fiscal year 2014 to oversee a "comprehensive and systematic risk management regime" across all bank operations (not just the portfolio). A prior reauthorization required an analysis of the potential for increased or decreased risk of loss to the bank as a result of rapid portfolio growth and changes in its composition.

Ethics

H.R. 597: The bill creates the position of chief ethics officer, and establishes an Office of Ethics under statute. The ethics officer is directed to draft a code of ethics. Bank employees must certify annually that they have "read, understand, and complied with and will continue to comply with the Code of Ethics" as well as the financial disclosures already required by law.

Current Policy: Ex-Im's Office of General Council is designated as the chief ethics official. Bank employees must comply with the Standards of Ethical Conduct for Employees of the Executive Branch and the Supplemental Standards of Ethical Conduct for Employees of the Export-Import Bank. Depending on position, they may also be subject to the Ethics in Government Act and the Foreign Corrupt Practices Act.

Fraud

H.R. 597: The bill requires the comptroller general every four years to review bank controls to prevent, detect, and investigate fraud, including an audit of sample transactions. Following the review, the comptroller general is required to submit a report of the findings to the House Committees on Financial Services and Appropriations, and the Senate Committees on Banking, Housing, and Urban Affairs, and Appropriations.

Current Policy: The bank must set due-diligence standards and require all delegated lenders to implement "Know Your Customer" practices. The comptroller general must review the adequacy of the due-diligence standards and submit the findings to Congress.

Information Technology

H.R. 597: The bill permits the expenditure of a portion of funds available for administrative expenses to improve Ex-Im's systems infrastructure.

Current Policy: The bank is permitted to use an amount equal to 1.25 percent of the surplus of the bank to remedy operational weaknesses in the information technology system.

Audits

H.R. 597: The bill requires the comptroller general to conduct an annual audit of Ex-Im programs. It also directs the board's Audit Committee to develop a program for routine audits.

Current Policy: The comptroller general conducts periodic audits of bank programs to determine compliance with underwriting guidelines, lending policies, due-diligence procedures and content guidelines. The comptroller general also reviews the adequacy of fraud controls and submits a report and recommendations to Congress.

Private Finance

H.R. 597: The bill directs the Federal Reserve Board to issue semiannual reports to Congress on the terms and conditions of private-export financing. Ex-Im Bank officials must issue annual reports to Congress on the steps taken to avoid crowding out private financing. Applicants (other than foreign banks) must demonstrate that they have unsuccessfully sought to obtain competitive financing, or that there is financing available to the applicant from a foreign export credit agency for comparable foreign goods and services.

Current Policy: Ex-Im, in the exercise of its functions, is directed to supplement and encourage, and not compete with, private capital. The bank is also directed to consider the need to involve private capital, as well as the cost of the transaction compared to private financing. The bank must accord equal opportunity to export agents and managers, independent export firms, export-trading companies, and small commercial banks in the formulation and implementation of its programs. The bank is supposed to direct its efforts toward financing export transactions that are unlikely to proceed without Ex-Im support.

Ending Export-Credit Financing

H.R. 597: The bill calls on the U.S. President to initiate and pursue negotiations with both Organization for Economic Co-operation Development (OECD) and non-OECD countries to reduce, with the "possible" goal of eliminating, subsidized export financing programs within 10 years. The bill directs the President

ISSUE BRIEF | NO. 4355
FEBRUARY 24, 2015

to submit to Congress a strategy for ending all forms of government export subsidies, and to submit a report on the progress of negotiations to the Senate Committee on Banking, Housing, and Urban Affairs and the House Committee on Financial Services.

Current Policy: The Secretary of the Treasury is required to initiate and pursue negotiations with OECD and non-OECD countries to substantially reduce, with the ultimate goal of eliminating, subsidized export financing and other forms of export subsidies. The Treasury Secretary is also required to pursue negotiations with all countries that finance air carrier aircraft, with the goal of substantially reducing and, ultimately, eliminating, aircraft export credit financing (for all aircraft covered by the 2007 Sector Understanding on Export Credits for Civil Aircraft).[15] The Secretary is obligated to submit a report on the progress of negotiations to the Senate Committee on Banking, Housing, and Urban Affairs and the House Committee on Financial Services.

In spite of the "reforms" instituted by previous Congresses—reforms that mirror those in H.R. 597—Ex-Im has failed to fully comply with risk-management standards. There has been a recent uptick in allegations of serious misconduct by Ex-Im Bank employees. The Office of Inspector General has identified deficiencies in internal controls that reduce the reliability of the bank to ferret out improper payments. There also are weaknesses in the bank's "Character, Reputational, Transactional Integrity" screening of applicants, as well as a pattern of insufficient due diligence by delegated lenders, specifically lenders with a history of defaulted transactions.

It may seem understandable that lawmakers regard Ex-Im as helpful to the businesses in their district. They would do well to consider the various drawbacks related to the subsidies, including distortions in the distribution of labor and capital, higher consumer costs, and the disadvantages to domestic firms that do not receive the subsidies that flow to their foreign competitors. In sum, it is time to recognize the huge difference between support for big business and support for free enterprise.

—Diane Katz is a Research Fellow for Regulatory Policy in the Thomas A. Roe Institute for Economic Policy Studies, of the Institute for Economic Freedom and Opportunity, at The Heritage Foundation.

---

15. OECD, "Sector Understanding on Export Credits for Civil Aircraft," July 27, 2007, http://www.oecd.org/officialdocuments/publicdisplaydocumentpdf/?cote=tad/pg(2007)4/FINAL&doclanguage=en (accessed February 20, 2015).